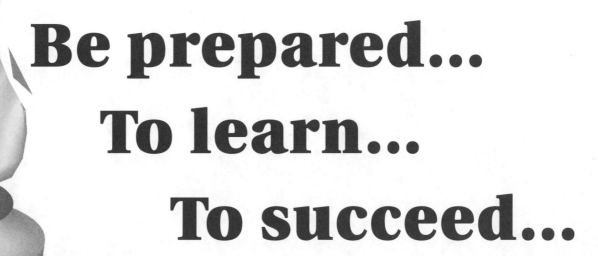

Be prepared...
To learn...
To succeed...

Get **REA**dy. It all starts here. REA's preparation for the MCAS is **fully aligned** with the Curriculum Framework Standards adopted by the Massachusetts State Board of Education.

Visit us online at
www.rea.com

READY, SET, GO!

Massachusetts

MCAS

Grade 7
English Language Arts

Staff of Research & Education Association

Research & Education Association
Visit our website at
www.rea.com

The Curriculum Framework Standards in this book
were created and implemented by the Massachusetts
Board of Education. For further information,
visit the Department of Education website at
http://www.doe.mass.edu/mcas/.

"Space Colonization" photo (p. 103) courtesy NASA

"Funnel Web" photo (p. 118) by Amit Kulkarni

"Sheet Web" photo (p. 118) by Alan Bauer

Research & Education Association
61 Ethel Road West
Piscataway, New Jersey 08854
E-mail: info@rea.com

Ready, Set, Go!
MCAS English Language Arts, Grade 7

Printed in the United States of America

Library of Congress Control Number 2006924032

International Standard Book Number 0-7386-0238-8

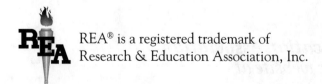

REA® is a registered trademark of
Research & Education Association, Inc.

TABLE OF CONTENTS

PART A: COMPOSITION

About Research & Education Association

Founded in 1959, Research & Education Association is dedicated to publishing the finest and most effective educational materials—including software, study guides, and test preps—for students in middle school, high school, college, graduate school, and beyond. Today, REA's wide-ranging catalog is a leading resource for teachers, students, and professionals.

We invite you to visit us at *www.rea.com* to find out how "REA is making the world smarter."

Acknowledgments

We would like to thank Larry B. Kling, Vice President, Editorial, for his editorial direction; Pam Weston, Vice President, Publishing, for setting the quality standards for production integrity and managing the publication to completion; Christine Reilley, Senior Editor, for project management; Diane Goldschmidt, Associate Editor, for post-production quality assurance; Christine Saul, Senior Graphic Artist, for cover design; Jeremy Rech, Graphic Artist, for interior page design; and Jeff LoBalbo, Senior Graphic Artist, for post-production file mapping.

We also gratefully acknowledge the writers, educators, and editors of REA, Northeast Editing, and Publication Services for content development, editorial guidance, and final review.

SUCCEEDING ON THE MCAS

ABOUT THIS BOOK

This book provides excellent preparation for the Massachusetts Comprehensive Assessment System (MCAS)—Grade 7 English Language Arts. Inside you will find exercises designed to provide students with the instruction, practice, and strategies needed to do well on this achievement test.

This book is divided into several parts: a **pretest**, which introduces students to the sections on the actual test, including

- short, long, and longer length reading selections

- multiple-choice and extended-response questions

- a writing composition section

Following the pretest is a lesson section, which teaches students about the different types of MCAS questions on the reading test, step by step. Students will begin with shorter selections and easier questions and conclude each lesson by completing full-length selections and questions modeled after those on the MCAS. Answer explanations are provided for each question in each lesson. "Tips" are also given below each question to guide students toward answering the question correctly. Finally, this book includes a full-length **posttest**, which matches the MCAS test in terms of content.

Begin by assigning students the pretest. Answers and answer explanations follow the pretest. Then work through each of the lessons one by one. When students have completed the book, they should complete the posttest. Answers and answer explanations follow the posttest.

HOW TO USE THIS BOOK

FOR STUDENTS: To make getting through the book as easy as possible, we've included icons shown on the next page that highlight sections like lessons, questions, and answers. You'll find that our practice tests are very much like the actual MCAS you'll encounter on test day. The best way to prepare for a test is to practice, so we've included drills with answers throughout the book, and our two practice tests include detailed answers.

FOR PARENTS: Massachusetts has created grade-appropriate learning standards that are listed in the table in this introduction. Students need to meet these objectives as measured by the MCAS. Our book will help your child review and prepare for the English Language Arts exam. It includes review sections, drills, and two practice tests complete with explanations to help your child focus on the areas he/she needs to work on to help master the test.

FOR TEACHERS: No doubt, you are already familiar with the MCAS and its format. Begin by assigning students the pretest, which is followed by an answer key and detailed explanations. Then work through each of the lessons in succession. When students have completed the subject review, they should move on to the posttest. Answers and answer explanations follow the posttest.

ICONS EXPLAINED

Icons make navigating through the book easier by highlighting sections like lessons, questions, and answers as explained below:

 Question

 Answer

 Tip

 Lesson

 Activity

 Writing Task

WHY STUDENTS ARE REQUIRED TO TAKE THE MCAS

MCAS measures the extent to which students are meeting the Massachusetts Curriculum Framework Standards. Massachusetts teachers and curriculum experts developed the MCAS in cooperation with the Massachusetts State Board of Education. The English Language Arts test is given to students in Grades 3, 5, and 7.

WHAT'S ON THE MCAS

The English Language Arts tests in Grade 7 are divided into two parts. Part A is the Composition Test, which uses a writing prompt to assess the learning standards. This part is given in two separate sessions, administered on the same day. The first session is comprised of writing an initial draft of a composition in response to the writing prompt. During the second session, the student will revise the original draft.

Part B is the Language and Literature Test, which includes three separate test sessions. Each session includes selected readings, followed by multiple-choice and open-response questions.

MCAS ENGLISH LANGUAGE ARTS STANDARDS*

Language Strand

Standard 4: Vocabulary and Concept Development | Page Numbers

Students will understand and acquire new vocabulary and use it correctly in reading and writing. — 73, 93, 126

Determine the meanings of unfamiliar words using context clues (for example, *contrast or cause and effect stated in the text*).

Determine the meanings of unfamiliar words using knowledge of common Greek and Latin roots, suffixes, and prefixes.

Determine pronunciations, meanings, alternate word choices, parts of speech, or etymologies of words using dictionaries and thesauruses.

Reading and Literature Strand

Standard 8: Understanding a Text | Page Numbers

Students will identify basic facts and main ideas in a text and use them as the basis for interpretation. — 53, 73, 93, 108, 148

Use knowledge of genre characteristics to analyze a text.

Interpret mood in a text and give supporting evidence.

Identify evidence in a text used to support an argument.

Standard 12: Fiction | Page Numbers

Students will identify, analyze, and apply knowledge of the structure and elements of fiction and provide evidence from the text to support their understanding. — 53, 93, 126

Analyze the connections among setting, characterization, conflict, plot, and/or theme.

Analyze characters' personality traits, motivations, and interactions with others and give supporting evidence from their words, actions, or thoughts.

Analyze the ways characters change or interact with others over time and give supporting evidence from the text.

* The Curriculum Framework Standards in this table were created and implemented by the Massachusetts Board of Education. For further information, visit the Board of Education website at *www.doe.mass.edu/mcas/*.

Standard 13: Nonfiction

Standard 14: Poetry

Standard 15: Style and Language

Standard 16: Myth, Traditional Narrative, and Classical Literature

Students will identify, analyze, and apply knowledge of the themes, structure, and elements of myths, traditional narratives, and classical literature and provide evidence from the text to support their understanding.

Identify conventions in epic tales (for example, *the extended simile, the hero's tasks, special weapons, clothing, helpers*).

Identify and analyze similarities and differences in mythologies from different cultures (for example, *ideas of the afterlife, roles and characteristics of deities, types and purposes of myths*).

Standard 17: Dramatic Literature

Students will identify, analyze, and apply knowledge of the themes, structure, and elements of drama and provide evidence from the text to support their understanding.

Identify and analyze elements of setting, plot, and characterization in plays that are read, viewed, written, and/or performed.

Setting (for example, *place, historical period, time of day*)

Plot (for example, *exposition, conflict, rising action, falling action*)

Characterization (for example, *character motivations, actions, thoughts, development*)

Identify and analyze the similarities and differences in the presentations of setting, character, and plot in texts, plays, and films.

 TIPS FOR STUDENTS

Students can do plenty of things before and during the actual test to improve their test-taking performance. The good thing is that most of the tips described below are easy!

Preparing for the Test

Test Anxiety

Do you get nervous when your teacher talks about taking a test? A certain amount of anxiety is normal and it actually may help you prepare better for the test by getting you motivated. But too much anxiety is a bad thing and may keep you from properly preparing for the test. Here are some things to consider that may help relieve test anxiety:

- Share how you are feeling with your parents and your teachers. They may have ways of helping you deal with how you are feeling.

- Keep on top of your game. Are you behind in your homework and class assignments? A lot of your classwork-related anxiety and stress will simply go away if you keep up with your homework assignments and classwork. And then you can focus on the test with a clearer mind.

- Relax. Take a deep breath or two. You should do this especially if you get anxious while taking the test.

Study Tips & Taking the Test

- **Learn the Test's Format.** Don't be surprised. By taking a practice test ahead of time you'll know what the test looks like, how much time you will have, how many questions there are, and what kinds of questions are going to appear on it. Knowing ahead of time is much better than being surprised.

- **Read the Entire Question.** Pay attention to what kind of answer a question or word problem is looking for. Reread the question if it does not make sense to you, and try to note the parts of the question needed for figuring out the right answer.

- **Read All the Answers.** On a multiple-choice test, the right answer could also be the last answer. You won't know unless you read all the possible answers to a question.

- **It's Not a Guessing Game.** If you don't know the answer to a question, don't make an uneducated guess. And don't randomly pick just any answer either. As you read over each possible answer to a question, note any answers which are obviously wrong. Each obviously wrong answer you identify and eliminate greatly improves your chances at selecting the right answer.

- **Don't Get Stuck on Questions.** Don't spend too much time on any one question. Doing this takes away time from the other questions. Work on the easier questions first. Skip the really hard questions and come back to them if there is still enough time.

- **Accuracy Counts.** Make sure you record your answer in the correct space on your answer sheet. Fixing mistakes only takes time away from you.

- **Finished Early?** Use this time wisely and double-check your answers.

Sound Advice for Test Day

The Night Before. Getting a good night's rest keeps your mind sharp and focused for the test.

The Morning of the Test. Have a good breakfast. Dress in comfortable clothes. Keep in mind that you don't want to be too hot or too cold while taking the test. Get to school on time. Give yourself time to gather your thoughts and calm down before the test begins.

Three Steps for Taking the Test

1) **Read.** Read the entire question and then read all the possible answers.

2) **Answer.** Answer the easier questions first and then go back to the more difficult questions.

3) **Double-Check.** Go back and check your work if time permits.

TIPS FOR PARENTS

- Encourage your child to take responsibility for homework and class assignments. Help your child create a study schedule. Mark the test's date on a family calendar as a reminder for both of you.

- Talk to your child's teachers. Ask them for progress reports on an ongoing basis.

- Commend your child's study and test successes. Praise your child for successfully following a study schedule, for doing homework, and for any work done well.

- Test Anxiety. Your child may experience nervousness or anxiety about the test. You may even be anxious, too. Here are some helpful tips on dealing with a child's test anxiety:

  - Talk about the test openly and positively with your child. An ongoing dialogue not only can relieve your child's anxieties but also serves as a progress report of how your child feels about the test.

  - Form realistic expectations of your child's testing abilities.

  - Be a "Test Cheerleader." Your encouragement to do his or her best on the test can alleviate your child's test anxiety.

PRETEST

PRETEST

Part A: Composition

WRITING: SESSION 1

DIRECTIONS

For this first session of Part A, you will be asked to respond to a writing prompt. Plan and draft your answer on a separate piece of paper. If you finish ahead of time, do not go on to the next part of the test. Wait for your teacher to continue.

Writing Prompt

WRITING PROMPT

This year, two of your school's teachers have retired. To save money to build a new gymnasium, your principal has decided to offer instruction for several classes using distance education, meaning you would only "see" your teacher via a television screen when a video tape is played. When you complete assignments or take tests for these classes, the school secretary will mail them to your teacher, who will grade them and mail them back.

Write a letter to the editor of your school newspaper. Explain your views on the principal's decision requiring some classes to be taught using distance education. Use examples, facts, and other evidence to support your point of view.

PREWRITING/PLANNING SPACE

DIRECTIONS
When you finish your planning, write your first draft on the lined page that follows.

Part A: Composition

REVISING: SESSION 2

DIRECTIONS

To complete this part of the test, you will revise and edit the draft you wrote in the first session. Copy your final draft on the lined page that follows.

Part B

LANGUAGE AND LITERATURE: SESSION 1

DIRECTIONS
This session contains reading selections with multiple-choice questions and open-response questions. Mark your answers to these questions on the Answer Sheets provided.

Introduction: This article discusses a change that the author believes needs to be made in school libraries.

Loose Laws in School Libraries
Schools Need to Protect Their Students

1　Censorship in school libraries has been the subject of much recent debate. Recently, a sixth-grade student at Gerald Hoover Middle School in California was scanning the school library's shelves for reference materials for a research paper when she came across a book containing graphic images inappropriate for children. The student was disturbed by these images and presented the book to the school librarian, who simply re-shelved the book and dismissed the student's concerns. Many parents feel that the school's response to this student's concerns is insufficient and irresponsible.

2　While the issue of censorship is a heated one with many different sides, responsible adults should monitor the materials that children have access to while in school. This does not mean that we need library-wide censorship. Public libraries have a duty to follow the Library Bill of Rights and provide readers with a wide range of materials. Though students may access materials considered inappropriate for children at the public library, it is not the library's responsibility to monitor what children are reading—it is the parents' responsibility. Parents can accompany their children into the public library and help them choose reading materials that they consider appropriate for their children. Parents cannot, however, do this in school libraries, and this is where the school, as a responsible educational institution, must step in.

3　Parents send their children off to school every day with the knowledge that they will be educated, protected, and cared for to the best of the school's ability. Schools do not allow harmful materials such as weapons or illegal substances, and they should not allow harmful reading materials either. When parents brought their personal concerns to the Gerald Hoover Middle School librarian, she told them that preventing students from accessing certain reading materials would be an abuse of their rights. However, if children have the right to view whatever materials have been made available to them, then this right must be abused in order to protect them. Many American laws are designed to protect those not old enough to make intelligent informed decisions, those who have not lived long enough or gained enough world experience to be responsible for themselves. When our children age and mature, they are given more freedom to make their own choices based on what they have learned while under our protective wings. Reading materials loaded with mature subject matter should be reserved for mature people, not sixth- and seventh-grade students.

4　Children see things much differently than adults do. When children view materials intended for adults, they are looking at the pictures and interpreting the text through a child's limited worldview. They do not always have the intellectual or emotional capacity to understand what they are reading. An adult reading the same text is much better equipped to interpret and understand the mature subject matter. The same principle applies to different forms of information and entertainment, such as television shows, movies, and video games, which all have content that is rated according to its appropriateness for different age groups. Many shows and movies containing graphic violence or nudity are deemed inappropriate for children, who cannot always understand what they are seeing, or who may mimic what they see. Most people agree that not every television program, movie, or video game is suitable for young children, so why are books different? Do librarians and educators truly believe that no book could harm a child, simply because it is a book? If certain images and subject matters are considered inappropriate in their video form, then why are they acceptable for children when put into print form? If children are not emotionally or intellectually mature enough to handle what they encounter, the results can be harmful and severe.

5   As previously stated, monitoring reading materials in a public library is a parent's job. When children are not in school, their parents are responsible for looking after them and caring for them. Because parents cannot accompany their children to school, school educators and administrators must step into many of the roles and responsibilities undertaken by parents. Students are fed, provided with intellectual and physical activities, and disciplined when necessary, so why, then, should the school be exempt from the responsibility of monitoring the reading materials to which our children are exposed? Should all concerned parents pull their students out of schools and educate them at home so that they are protected in a way that the schools cannot—or will not—do? This is not the best answer, but it shows that when schools will not take responsibility for protecting their students, some type of parental action is necessary.

6   The inappropriate materials on the shelves of school libraries should be formally reviewed, beginning with the one book that we know

has had a <u>detrimental</u> effect on at least one of the school's students—the one that still sits on the shelves of Gerald Hoover Middle School, available to all students. The school library has a materials selection policy, and the board of education makes the final decisions about library materials. While their intentions are likely good ones, they have obviously let a few inappropriate materials slip through the cracks, so parents cannot be sure that their children are not reading books too mature for their years. While academic and intellectual freedoms are important, they are only beneficial to children when exercised responsibly, and those running the school in question have proven themselves irresponsible in this respect. Perhaps school libraries need additional safeguards on mature materials, such as a separate section of the library for mature materials, which students would need to present identification verifying their ages in order to enter. Or perhaps schools need to put control back into the hands of the parents by requiring parents to sign a form stating whether or not their child is permitted to access mature materials in the school library. Whatever the answer, it is clear that change is necessary for the safety of schoolchildren.

1 "Loose Laws in School Libraries" is specifically about a struggle between

   happiness and maturity.

   fairness and success.

   rights and responsibilities.

   parents and schools.

2 Which detail supports the author's main idea?

   Libraries contain many types of books.

   Children need to be protected.

   Parents should supervise their children.

   Schools should not tell children what to read.

3 Though "Loose Laws in School Libraries" is about one person's thoughts on books in school libraries, it would be useful background material for an oral report on

   censorship in schools.

   education in California.

   regulations in public libraries.

   the best books for young adults.

4 In paragraph 1, why does the author tell the anecdote about the sixth-grade student at Gerald Hoover Middle School?

A. To show that some librarians do not care about students.

   To prove that libraries contain books meant for adults.

   To demonstrate that parents need to become more involved.

   To show that some books may upset students.

5 In paragraph 6, detrimental means

   reliable

   valuable

   harmful

   spiteful

6 The phrase "slip through the cracks" in paragraph 6 means that

A. something unwanted has gotten through defenses.

B. the library floor needs repair.

C. some library materials are very narrow.

D. someone in the library has slipped and fallen on the job.

Write your answer to open-response question 7 in the space provided in the Answer Sheets.

7 In "Loose Laws in School Libraries" the author discusses how books should be selected for school libraries.

- Give one example of a book you have read that should definitely be included in school libraries.
- Do you think the author of this article would agree with your choice? Why or why not?

Use information from the article to support your answer.

Read this poem. Think about its main idea as you read. When you finish reading the poem, answer the questions that follow.

Because I could not stop for Death
Emily Dickinson

Because I could not stop for Death—
He kindly stopped for me—
The Carriage held but just Ourselves—
And Immortality.

We slowly drove—He knew no haste
And I had put away
My labor and my leisure too,
For His Civility—

We passed the School, where Children strove
At Recess—in the Ring—
We passed the Fields of Gazing Grain—
We passed the Setting Sun—

Or rather—He passed us—
The Dews drew quivering and chill—
For only Gossamer, my Gown—
My Tippet—only Tulle—

We paused before a House that seemed
A Swelling of the Ground—
The Roof was scarcely visible—
The Cornice—in the Ground—

Since then— 'tis Centuries—and yet
Feels shorter than the Day
I first surmised the Horses' Heads
Were toward Eternity—

8 This poem is mostly about

A. how a woman learns that she is not immortal.

B. a woman who takes a carriage ride with a polite man.

C. how death comes for a woman who did not expect it.

D. a woman who takes the time to remember the events of her life.

9 What does the woman pass after the Fields of Gazing Grain?

A. a Ring

B. some Children

C. the Setting Sun

D. a School

10 Where does the woman think she is headed at first?

A. Eternity

B. Immortality

C. the School

D. a Cornice in the Ground

LANGUAGE AND LITERATURE: SESSION 2

DIRECTIONS

This session contains a reading selection with multiple-choice questions and one open-response question. Mark your answers to these questions on the Answer Sheets provided.

INTRODUCTION: In this excerpt from the novel The Secret Garden, *Mary and her friend Dickon consider taking Colin, an injured boy who also seems to be paralyzed, to see a garden that they consider to be their secret place.*

The Secret Garden
by Frances Hodgson Burnett
(from Chapter 15—"Nest Building")

1   After another week of rain the high arch of blue sky appeared again and the sun which poured down was quite hot. Though there had been no chance to see either the secret garden or Dickon, Mistress Mary had enjoyed herself very much. The week had not seemed long. She had spent hours of every day with Colin in his room, talking about Rajahs or gardens or Dickon and the cottage on the moor. They had looked at the splendid books and pictures and sometimes Mary had read things to Colin, and sometimes he had read a little to her. When he was amused and interested she thought he scarcely looked like an invalid at all, except that his face was so colorless and he was always on the sofa. . . .

2   In her talks with Colin, Mary had tried to be very cautious about the secret garden. There were certain things she wanted to find out from him, but she felt that she must find them out without asking him direct questions. In the first place, as she began to like to be with him, she wanted to discover whether he was the kind of boy you could tell a secret to. He was not in the least like Dickon, but he was evidently so pleased with the idea of a garden no one knew anything about that she thought perhaps he could be trusted. But she had not known him long enough to be sure. The second thing she wanted to find out was this: If he could be trusted–if he really could–wouldn't it be possible to take him to the garden without having anyone find it out? The grand doctor had said that he must have fresh air and Colin had said that he would not mind fresh air in a secret garden. Perhaps if he had a great deal of fresh air and knew Dickon and the robin and saw things growing he might not think so much about dying. Mary had seen herself in the glass sometimes lately when she had realized that she looked quite a different creature from the child she had seen when she arrived from India. This child looked nicer. Even Martha had seen a change in her.

3   "Th' air from th' moor has done thee good already," she had said. "Tha'rt not nigh so yeller and tha'rt not nigh so scrawny. Even tha' hair doesn't slamp down on tha' head so flat. It's got some life in it so as it sticks out a bit."

4   "It's like me," said Mary. "It's growing stronger and fatter. I'm sure there's more of it."

5   "It looks it, for sure," said Martha, ruffling it up a little round her face. "Tha'rt not half so ugly when it's that way an' there's a bit o' red in tha' cheeks."

6   If gardens and fresh air had been good for her perhaps they would be good for Colin. But then, if he hated people to look at him, perhaps he would not like to see Dickon.

7   "Why does it make you angry when you are looked at?" she inquired one day.

8   "I always hated it," he answered, "even when I was very little. Then when they took me to the seaside and I used to lie in my carriage everybody used to stare and ladies would stop and talk to my nurse and then they would begin to whisper and I knew then they were saying I shouldn't live to grow up. Then sometimes the ladies would pat my cheeks and say 'Poor child!' Once when a lady did that I screamed out loud and bit her hand. She was so frightened she ran away."

9   "She thought you had gone mad like a dog," said Mary, not at all admiringly.

10   "I don't care what she thought," said Colin, frowning.

11   "I wonder why you didn't scream and bite me when I came into your room?" said Mary. Then she began to smile slowly.

12   "I thought you were a ghost or a dream," he said. "You can't bite a ghost or a dream, and if you scream they don't care."

13   "Would you hate it if–if a boy looked at you?" Mary asked uncertainly.

14   He lay back on his cushion and paused thoughtfully.

15   "There's one boy," he said quite slowly, as if he were thinking over every word, "there's one boy I believe I shouldn't mind. It's that boy who knows where the foxes live–Dickon."

***

16   On that first morning when the sky was blue again Mary wakened very early. The sun was pouring in slanting rays through the blinds and there was something so joyous in the sight of it that she jumped out of bed and ran to the window. She drew up the blinds and opened the window itself and a great waft of fresh, scented air blew in upon her. The moor was blue and the whole world looked as if something magic had happened to it. There were tender little fluting sounds here and there and everywhere, as if scores of birds were beginning to tune up for a concert. Mary put her hand out of the window and held it in the sun.

17   "It's warm–warm!" she said. "It will make the green points push up and up and up, and it will make the bulbs and roots work and struggle with all their might under the earth."

18   She kneeled down and leaned out of the window as far as she could, breathing big breaths and sniffing the air until she laughed because she remembered what Dickon's mother had said about the end of his nose quivering like a rabbit's. "It must be very early," she said. "The little clouds are all pink and I've never seen the sky look like this. No one is up. I don't even hear the stable boys."

19   A sudden thought made her scramble to her feet.

20   "I can't wait! I am going to see the garden!"

21   She had learned to dress herself by this time and she put on her clothes in five minutes. She knew a small side door which she could unbolt herself and she flew downstairs in her stocking feet and put on her shoes in the hall. She unchained and unbolted and unlocked and when the door was open she sprang across the step with one bound, and there she was standing on the grass, which seemed to have turned green, and with the sun pouring down on her and warm sweet wafts about her and the fluting and twittering and singing coming from every bush and tree. She clasped her hands for pure joy and looked up in the sky and it was so blue and pink and pearly and white and flooded with springtime light that she felt as if she must flute and sing aloud herself and knew that thrushes and robins and skylarks could not possibly help it. She ran around the shrubs and paths towards the secret garden.

22   "It is all different already," she said. "The grass is greener and things are sticking up everywhere and things are uncurling and green buds of leaves are showing. This afternoon I am sure Dickon will come."

23   The long warm rain had done strange things to the herbaceous beds which bordered the walk by

the lower wall. There were things sprouting and pushing out from the roots of clumps of plants and there were actually here and there glimpses of royal purple and yellow unfurling among the stems of crocuses. Six months before Mistress Mary would not have seen how the world was waking up, but now she missed nothing.

24 When she had reached the place where the door hid itself under the ivy, she was startled by a curious loud sound. It was the caw–caw of a crow and it came from the top of the wall, and when she looked up, there sat a big glossy-plumaged blue-black bird, looking down at her very wisely indeed. She had never seen a crow so close before and he made her a little nervous, but the next moment he spread his wings and flapped away across the garden. She hoped he was not going to stay inside and she pushed the door open wondering if he would. When she got fairly into the garden she saw that he probably did intend to stay because he had alighted on a dwarf apple-tree and under the apple-tree was lying a little reddish animal with a Bushy tail, and both of them were watching the stooping body and rust-red head of Dickon, who was kneeling on the grass working hard.

25 Mary flew across the grass to him.

26 "Oh, Dickon! Dickon!" she cried out. "How could you get here so early! How could you! The sun has only just got up!"

27 He got up himself, laughing and glowing, and tousled; his eyes like a bit of the sky.

28 "Eh!" he said. "I was up long before him. How could I have stayed abed! Th' world's all fair begun again this mornin', it has. An' it's workin' an' hummin' an' scratchin' an' pipin' an' nest-buildin' an' breathin' out scents, till you've got to be out on it 'stead o' lyin' on your back. When th' sun did jump up, th' moor went mad for joy, an' I was in the midst of th' heather, an' I run like mad myself, shoutin' an' singin'. An' I come straight here. I couldn't have stayed away. Why, th' garden was lyin' here waitin'!"

29 Mary put her hands on her chest, panting, as if she had been running herself.

30 "Oh, Dickon! Dickon!" she said. "I'm so happy I can scarcely breathe!"

31 Seeing him talking to a stranger, the little bushy-tailed animal rose from its place under the tree and came to him, and the rook, cawing once, flew down from its branch and settled quietly on his shoulder.

32 "This is th' little fox cub," he said, rubbing the little reddish animal's head. "It's named Captain. An' this here's Soot. Soot he flew across th' moor with me an' Captain he run same as if th' hounds had been after him. They both felt same as I did."

33 Neither of the creatures looked as if he were the least afraid of Mary. When Dickon began to walk about, Soot stayed on his shoulder and Captain trotted quietly close to his side.

34 "See here!" said Dickon. "See how these has pushed up, an' these an' these! An' Eh! Look at these here!"

35 He threw himself upon his knees and Mary went down beside him. They had come upon a whole clump of crocuses burst into purple and orange and gold. Mary bent her face down and kissed and kissed them. . . . There was every joy on earth in the secret garden that morning, and in the midst of them came a delight more delightful than all, because it was more wonderful. Swiftly something flew across the wall and darted through the trees to a close grown corner, a little flare of red-breasted bird with something hanging from its beak. Dickon stood quite still and put his hand on Mary almost as if they had suddenly found themselves laughing in a church.

36 "We munnot stir," he whispered in broad Yorkshire. "We munnot scarce breathe. I knowed he was mate-huntin' when I seed him last. It's Ben Weatherstaff's robin. He's buildin' his nest. He'll stay here if us don't fright him." They settled down softly upon the grass and sat there without moving.

37 "Us mustn't seem as if us was watchin' him too close," said Dickon. "He'd be out with us for good if he got th' notion us was interferin' now. . . . He's settin' up housekeepin'. He'll

be shyer an' readier to take things ill. He's got no time for visitin' an' gossipin'. Us must keep still a bit an' try to look as if us was grass an' trees an' bushes. Then when he's got used to seein' us I'll chirp a bit an' he'll know us'll not be in his way."

38   Mistress Mary was not at all sure that she knew, as Dickon seemed to, how to try to look like grass and trees and bushes. But he had said the queer thing as if it were the simplest and most natural thing in the world, and she felt it must be quite easy to him, and indeed she watched him for a few minutes carefully, wondering if it was possible for him to quietly turn green and put out branches and leaves. But he only sat wonderfully still, and when he spoke dropped his voice to such a softness that it was curious that she could hear him, but she could.

39   "It's part o' th' springtime, this nest-buildin' is," he said. "I warrant it's been goin' on in th' same way every year since th' world was begun. They've got their way o' thinkin' and doin' things an' a body had better not meddle. You can lose a friend in springtime easier than any other season if you're too curious."

40   "If we talk about him I can't help looking at him," Mary said as softly as possible. "We must talk of something else. There is something I want to tell you."

41   "He'll like it better if us talks o' somethin' else," said Dickon. "What is it tha's got to tell me?"

42   "Well–do you know about Colin?" she whispered.

43   He turned his head to look at her.

44   "What does tha' know about him?" he asked.

45   "I've seen him. I have been to talk to him every day this week. He wants me to come. He says I'm making him forget about being ill and dying," answered Mary.

46   Dickon looked actually relieved as soon as the surprise died away from his round face.

47   "I am glad o' that," he exclaimed. "I'm right down glad. It makes me easier. I knowed I must say nothin' about him an' I don't like havin' to hide things."

48   "Don't you like hiding the garden?" said Mary.

49   "I'll never tell about it," he answered. "But I says to mother, 'Mother,' I says, 'I got a secret to keep. It's not a bad 'un, tha' knows that. It's no worse than hidin' where a bird's nest is. Tha' doesn't mind it, does tha'?'"

50   Mary always wanted to hear about mother.

51   "What did she say?" she asked, not at all afraid to hear.

52   Dickon grinned sweet-temperedly.

53   "It was just like her, what she said," he answered. "She give my head a bit of a rub an' laughed an' she says, 'Eh, lad, tha' can have all th' secrets tha' likes. I've knowed thee twelve year'.'"

54   "How did you know about Colin?" asked Mary.

55   "Everybody as knowed about Mester Craven knowed there was a little lad as was like to be a cripple, an' they knowed Mester Craven didn't like him to be talked about. Folks is sorry for Mester Craven because Mrs. Craven was such a pretty young lady an' they was so fond of each other. Mrs. Medlock stops in our cottage whenever she goes to Thwaite an' she doesn't mind talkin' to mother before us children, because she knows us has been brought up to be trusty. How did tha' find out about him? Martha was in fine trouble th' last time she came home. She said tha'd heard him frettin' an' tha' was askin' questions an' she didn't know what to say."

***

56   "Colin's so afraid of it himself that he won't sit up," said Mary. "He says he's always thinking that if he should feel a lump coming he should go crazy and scream himself to death."

57   "Eh! he oughtn't to lie there thinkin' things like that," said Dickon. "No lad could get well as thought them sort o' things."

58   The fox was lying on the grass close by him, looking up to ask for a pat now and then, and Dickon bent down and rubbed his neck softly and thought a few minutes in silence. Presently he lifted his head and looked round the garden.

59   "When first we got in here," he said, "it seemed like everything was gray. Look round now and tell me if tha' doesn't see a difference."

60   Mary looked and caught her breath a little.

61   "Why!" she cried, "the gray wall is changing. It is as if a green mist were creeping over it. It's almost like a green gauze veil."

62   "Aye," said Dickon. "An' it'll be greener and greener till th' gray's all gone. Can tha' guess what I was thinkin'?"

63   "I know it was something nice," said Mary eagerly. "I believe it was something about Colin."

64   "I was thinkin' that if he was out here he wouldn't be watchin' for lumps to grow on his back; he'd be watchin' for buds to break on th' rose-bushes, an' he'd likely be healthier," explained Dickon. "I was wonderin' if us could ever get him in th' humor to come out here an' lie under th' trees in his carriage."

65   "I've been wondering that myself. I've thought of it almost every time I've talked to him," said Mary. "I've wondered if he could keep a secret and I've wondered if we could bring him here without any one seeing us. I thought perhaps you could push his carriage. The doctor said he must have fresh air and if he wants us to take him out no one dare disobey him. He won't go out for other people and perhaps they will be glad if he will go out with us. He could order the gardeners to keep away so they wouldn't find out."

66   Dickon was thinking very hard as he scratched Captain's back.

67   "It'd be good for him, I'll warrant," he said. "Us'd not be thinkin' he'd better never been born.

Us'd be just two children watchin' a garden grow, an' he'd be another. Two lads an' a little lass just lookin' on at th' springtime. I warrant it'd be better than doctor's stuff."

68   "He's been lying in his room so long and he's always been so afraid of his back that it has made him queer," said Mary. "He knows a good many things out of books but he doesn't know anything else. He says he has been too ill to notice things and he hates going out of doors and hates gardens and gardeners. But he likes to hear about this garden because it is a secret. I daren't tell him much but he said he wanted to see it."

69   "Us'll have him out here sometime for sure," said Dickon. "I could push his carriage well enough. Has tha' noticed how th' robin an' his mate has been workin' while we've been sittin' here? Look at him perched on that branch wonderin' where it'd be best to put that twig he's got in his beak."

70   He made one of his low whistling calls and the robin turned his head and looked at him inquiringly, still holding his twig. Dickon spoke to him as Ben Weatherstaff did, but Dickon's tone was one of friendly advice. . . .

71   "Tha' knows us won't trouble thee," he said to the robin. "Us is near bein' wild things ourselves. Us is nest-buildin' too, bless thee. Look out tha' doesn't tell on us."

72   And though the robin did not answer, because his beak was occupied, Mary knew that when he flew away with his twig to his own corner of the garden the darkness of his dew-bright eye meant that he would not tell their secret for the world.

11 Why doesn't Mary tell Colin about the secret garden at first?

A. She is not sure she can trust him.

B. She is not sure he is well enough.

C. She does not think he will like Dickon.

D. She does not know if he wants to see it.

12 Which of the following contributes MOST to Dickon's unusual character?

A. He has bright red hair and blue eyes.

B. He is excited about meeting Colin.

C. He communicates with wild animals.

D. He likes to spend time in the secret garden.

13 At the end of the passage, which BEST describes the narrator's tone?

A. suspenseful

B. mysterious

C. playful

D. humorous

14 The author writes Martha's and Dickon's speech differently ("Th'air," "Tha'rt," "tha'") because he wants to show that they

A. should not be trusted.

B. have speech impediments.

C. are dumb.

D. come from a different class and background.

15 Which experience would BEST help you to understand Mary's dilemma?

A. traveling to a new place

B. making a new friend

C. enjoying a spring day

D. taking care of a pet

16 In paragraph 24, the author writes that the crow "had alighted on a dwarf apple-tree." What does <u>alighted</u> mean?

A. flown by

B. squawked at

C. crawled on

D. landed on

17 At what point in the story does Dickon decide to tell Mary that he knows about Colin?

A. When his mother tells him that it is okay to keep some secrets.

B. When he sees Mary entering the secret garden.

C. When Mary says that she has been spending time with Colin.

D. When Mary says that Colin is afraid to sit up.

18 In paragraph 52, "sweet-temperedly" is used as

A. an adverb to describe how Dickon grinned.

B. an adjective to describe Dickon.

C. a noun to stand for Dickon

D. a prepositional phrase.

19 Martha thinks that Mary looks better because

A. she is smiling.

B. she is thinner.

C. her hair is thicker.

D. her cheeks are rosy.

Write your answer to open-response question 20 in the space provided in the Answer Sheets.

 Throughout the story, Mary and Dickon do not want others to learn about the secret garden. If you were Mary or Dickon

   •   would you tell others about the secret garden?

   •   why or why not?

Use information from the story to support your answer.

ANSWER SHEETS

Part B: Language and Literature

SESSION 1

1. Ⓐ   Ⓑ   Ⓒ   Ⓓ

2. Ⓐ   Ⓑ   Ⓒ   Ⓓ

3. Ⓐ   Ⓑ   Ⓒ   Ⓓ

4. Ⓐ   Ⓑ   Ⓒ   Ⓓ

5. Ⓐ   Ⓑ   Ⓒ   Ⓓ

6. Ⓐ   Ⓑ   Ⓒ   Ⓓ

7. _____

   _____

   _____

   _____

   _____

   _____

   _____

8. Ⓐ   Ⓑ   Ⓒ   Ⓓ

9. Ⓐ   Ⓑ   Ⓒ   Ⓓ

10. Ⓐ   Ⓑ   Ⓒ   Ⓓ

SESSION 1

11. Ⓐ Ⓑ Ⓒ Ⓓ

12. Ⓐ Ⓑ Ⓒ Ⓓ

13. Ⓐ Ⓑ Ⓒ Ⓓ

14. Ⓐ Ⓑ Ⓒ Ⓓ

15. Ⓐ Ⓑ Ⓒ Ⓓ

16. Ⓐ Ⓑ Ⓒ Ⓓ

17. Ⓐ Ⓑ Ⓒ Ⓓ

18. Ⓐ Ⓑ Ⓒ Ⓓ

19. Ⓐ Ⓑ Ⓒ Ⓓ

20. _____

_____

_____

_____

_____

_____

_____

_____

ANSWER KEY

Part A

WRITING: SESSIONS 1 AND 2

Sample answer:

To the editor:

    I am writing in response to Principal Snyder's decision to turn certain required classes into distance education classes. I think this is a horrible idea. I understand that the principal is trying to save money to build a new gym, but it seems that he's willing to do so by sacrificing the quality of our education.

    Since when is a videotape a good substitute for a teacher? With no teacher present to monitor students' progress, some students may get bored with the material quickly while others may have trouble keeping up. There will be no one there to gauge when it is appropriate to slow down or move on. What if we have questions about confusing material? If our teacher can only be seen on a videotape, there will be no one present to answer our questions and give us feedback on assignments and tests. There has to be a better way for the school district to save money than by reducing our teachers and classes to videotapes.

Sincerely,
Terrell Warner

Part B

LANGUAGE AND LITERATURE: SESSION 1

1.   C   (Reading/Nonfiction)

The article is specifically about a struggle between the rights of students and the responsibilities of adults. The author says that while students may have a right to read anything in print, adults have a responsibility to protect them from material written for adults, which might upset children.

2.   B   (Understanding a Text)

The main idea of the article is that some books are inappropriate for children and that adults need to protect them from the content in these books. Therefore, answer choice B, "Children need to be protected," is the best answer choice.

3.   A   (Reading/Nonfiction)

To answer this question correctly, consider what most of the article is about: keeping inappropriate reading materials out of school libraries. While the author's idea aims to protect students, it is a form of censorship. Therefore, most of the article is about censorship in schools and this is the best answer choice.

4.   D   (Style and Language)

The author tells the anecdote about the sixth-grade student at Gerald Hoover Middle School to show that the book upset the student. Therefore, answer choice D is the best answer.

5.   C   (Vocabulary Development)

The sentence in paragraph 6 that uses the word "detrimental" says, "The inappropriate materials on the shelves of school libraries should be formally reviewed, beginning with the one book that we know has had a detrimental effect on at least one of the school's students . . ." This student is the sixth-grader at Gerald Hoover Middle School. This student was upset, so detrimental means "harmful."

6.   A   (Style and Language)

The phrase means something has gotten through that shouldn't, despite good intentions. Choice A is the best answer.

7.   (Reading/Nonfiction)

Sample answer: The book *Huckleberry Finn* by Mark Twain should definitely be included in all school libraries. The book is a great read and gives readers a lot of insight into life in the South in the past. However, I think the author of "Loose Laws in School Libraries" might disagree with my recommendation because the book is about a rebellious young boy who runs away with a slave. The author might consider the subject matter and some of the language in the book inappropriate for younger readers.

8.   C   (Reading/Poetry)

While several of the answer choices seem as if they are correct, only one answer choice expresses the main idea of the poem: answer choice C. The woman, the speaker of the poem, says that she was too busy to stop for death, but that death kindly stopped for her.

9.   C   (Reading/Poetry)

The answer to this question is stated in the poem. Answer choice C is the answer that appears immediately after the Fields of Gazing Grain.

10.   A   (Reading/Poetry)

You need to reread the end of the poem to find this answer. It is stated in the poem.

LANGUAGE AND LITERATURE: SESSION 2

11.   A   (Understanding a Text)

In the beginning of the story, the narrator says that Mary is thinking about telling Colin about the garden, but she is not yet sure she can trust him. Therefore, answer choice A is the correct answer.

12.   C   (Style and Language)

This question asks you to identify the most unusual thing about Dickon. Dickon is petting a baby fox throughout the story and a crow perches on his shoulder. He also talks to a robin. His actions with animals contribute most to this unusual character. Therefore, answer choice C is the best answer.

13.   C   (Style and Language)

The end of the story describes Dickon talking to the robin and says that Mary believes the robin will keep their secret. It is not particularly suspenseful, mysterious, or humorous. It is playful, so answer choice C is correct.

14.   D   (Style and Language)

The author does not intend to make fun or belittle the characters. The author uses that spelling to develop character by showing their particular class in society, their economic background.

15.   B   (Reading/Fiction)

To answer this question correctly, you need to first consider what Mary's dilemma is. She is considering whether to take Colin to the garden and let him in on her secret. She does not know him all that well yet, however, and is not sure he can be trusted. Answer choice B is the best answer.

16.   D   (Vocabulary Development)

If you're not sure of the answer to this question, try substituting the answer choices into the sentence. If a bird "alighted" on a dwarf apple tree, it probably landed on it. Answer choice D is correct.

17.   C   (Understanding a Text)

Dickon only confesses that he knows about Colin after Mary admits she has been spending time with him. Therefore, answer choice C is correct.

18.   A   (Style and Language)

"Sweet-temperedly" is used as an adverb (the "ly" is a clue) to describe (modify) the way the character grinned (a verb).

19.   D   (Reading/Fiction)

In the beginning of the story, Martha says that Mary looks better because she has gained weight and has rosy cheeks. Therefore, answer choice D is correct.

20.   (Reading/Fiction)

Sample answer: If I were Mary or Dickon, I would not tell others about the secret garden. If they tell people how beautiful it is there, others will come to see it. Dickon has befriended many animals in the garden that might be scared off by newcomers. Telling others about the garden will only alter its beauty.

PART A:
Composition

In the next lessons you will practice writing and then revising short essays. On the MCAS, you will be asked to respond to a writing prompt by prewriting, drafting, and then revising. Your responses could be in one of these forms:

- **Analyze/Explain**—You will be asked to read a poem and answer a question about the poem. This type of writing prompt usually makes a statement about the poem and then asks you to respond to the statement. For example, it might say, "In this poem, the reader learns an important lesson. Think about a lesson you have learned. Write an explanation of this lesson and analyze why it was important to you."

- **Persuade**—You will be asked to respond to a writing prompt that gives you a situation by taking a stand and persuading readers to believe as you believe. You might be asked to write a letter to the editor about an issue affecting your community or a letter to the school board about a matter concerning your school.

Lesson 1: Writing

This lesson covers skills for writing a first draft of an essay in response to a writing prompt that:

- Is clearly organized

- Has a focus

- Includes adequate supporting details

- Uses appropriate language

Developing Your Essays: The Three Stages of Writing

As you begin to develop your essay, you should follow the three stages of writing: prewriting, drafting, and revising. On the MCAS, you may be presented with a picture and asked to speculate about what is happening in the picture. You might be asked to read a poem and analyze or explain the poem. Or you may be given an important issue and asked to explain whether you agree or disagree with the issue. No matter what type of essay you are writing, you should always begin to develop your essay by prewriting.

Prewriting—RECORD Your Ideas

The main purpose of prewriting is to record your ideas. You can do this by brainstorming what you will be writing about in your essay. Start by jotting down ideas and possible angles for your essay. Think about the positive and negative aspects of a topic. Think about the audience for whom you will be writing and the purpose of your writing. Are you writing to entertain readers with a story, give your opinion, or explain something? Once you have determined your central idea, purpose, and audience, write down some supporting material and organize or outline your ideas into a logical sequence.

Suppose your task is to write an essay in support of or against tearing down an old building:

At the last city council meeting, a local business owner asked the council members for permission to tear down a historic building on Main Street to build a new clothing store in its place. Council members were divided on the issue. Some argued that the building was built before the Civil War and had too much historic value to be destroyed. Others argued that the old building was nothing more than an eyesore and a safety hazard and that a new store would make the downtown area more attractive.

The mayor decided to postpone voting on the issue until she could hear more details about both sides of the issue. How do you feel about tearing down the historic building?

Write an essay giving your opinion on the issue. Use facts and examples to develop your argument.

How would you begin to prepare an essay on this issue? First, you would take a moment to jot down a few notes about the issue. Why is the old building important? What are the benefits of the new store? You would ask yourself how you feel about the issue. Do you disagree with tearing down the building or would you rather have a new clothing store? Once you decide on the angle you want to take in your essay, add some details to support your position. You could create a web to help develop your argument and organize your ideas.

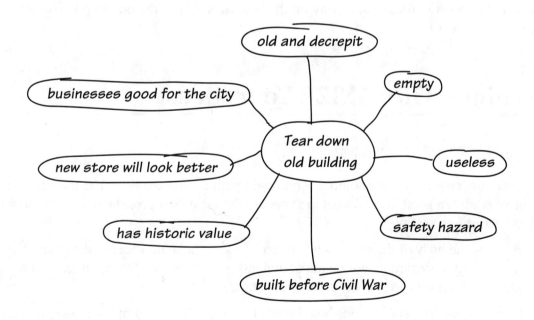

Prewriting—EVALUATE Your Ideas

When you have finished developing your argument, evaluate what you've written. Which ideas will help persuade the reader to share your opinion? Which ideas might weaken your argument? Don't be afraid to eliminate one or more of your ideas.

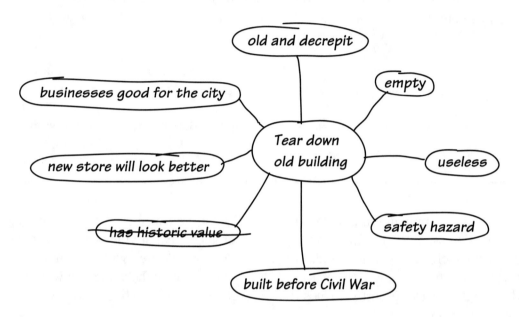

The fact that the building has historic value doesn't support the argument to tear it down. You probably wouldn't want to focus your essay on the historic value of the building if you were trying to convince readers to tear it down.

Prewriting—ORGANIZE Your Ideas

A good essay is organized into three parts:

1. Introduction—An essay should always begin with an introduction. The introduction should give readers a good idea of what to expect in the essay and give them a clue as to why you are writing the essay.

2. Body—The body of the essay is where you present the main ideas of the essay. Your main ideas, or in this example your main arguments, should be clearly explained. State your main ideas or opinions and support them with details.

3. Conclusion—The conclusion should provide a quick summary of your essay and leave the reader with your final word on the issue.

Drafting—Begin Your FIRST DRAFT

In the drafting stage of writing, you will write a rough draft of your work. An important thing to remember when writing your draft is to get your ideas down on paper. In this stage of writing, your writing does not have to be perfect. It is acceptable for the rough draft to have mistakes in grammar, spelling, and punctuation. These mistakes can be changed or fixed later.

Your first draft may look something like this:

I think that replacing the building with a new clothing store is a grate idea. At the last city council meeting a local business owner asked permishon to tear down the old building on Main St. The business owner wants to build a new clothing store in its place. I think city council should vote for this project.

Right now, the old building is full of broke windows. The doors are missing and bats and rats live their. More than anything, the building is an eye sore. A new building of any kind would look better.

Some city council members have argued that the old building is historic. Because it was built before the civil war. But, they fail to mention that the building has is in disrepare. Building a new store will improve the look of the downtown area. Pieces of broken glass and brick could easily fall to the ground and hurt people on the sidewalk the building is just not safe.

Finally, the old building is empty and useless. Bilding a new store in it's place would bring more people and more money into the city. It's taking up a lot of space and it's not being used for anything.

> I would like to ask all city council members to think about how wonderful Main St. could look if the unsafe, useless, eyesore of a building was torn down. And replaced with a brand new store.

Revising and Editing—Preparing the FINAL DRAFT

After you write your rough draft, it's time to begin revising and editing your work. Read your rough draft carefully. Look for mistakes in grammar, spelling, punctuation, and capitalization. Look for sentence fragments. Make sure that you have stated your main idea or that you have provided enough supporting details for readers to determine the central theme. Reword sentences or move entire paragraphs to make your writing flow in a clear, logical order. Add more details to make your writing vibrant and exciting.

Editorial Symbols

When you edit your first draft, you will find it helpful to use editorial symbols. These are marks on the page that show how you want your composition to be improved. The most common editorial symbols are

✐	This is a delete symbol. It tells you what should be removed from the text.
∧	This is an insert symbol. It tells you what should be added to the text.
⊙	This symbol tells you to add a period.
=	This mark under a letter means that it should be changed to an uppercase letter.
/	This mark through a letter tells you that it should be changed to a lowercase letter.
‿	This symbol means that you should delete a word or space and bring the surrounding letters together.

When you have finished revising your first draft, refer to the Writer's Checklist to help perfect your essay. Make sure that your essay hits each point listed in the following Writer's Checklist. Then write the final copy of your work in the answer booklet of your test.

Writer's Checklist

_____   Focus on the main idea of your writing and think about your audience.

_____   Support your main idea with interesting facts and details.

_____   Organize your ideas in a logical sequence that best communicates what you are trying to say.

_____   Vary the length and structure of your sentences.

_____   Know the meanings of the words you choose, and use them correctly.

_____   Check the basics. Make sure your capitalization, punctuation, and spelling are correct.

_____   Use your best handwriting for the final copy of your writing.

The final draft of your essay might look something like this:

At the last city council meeting, a local business owner asked permission to tear down the old building on Main Street and construct a new clothing store in its place. I think that replacing the old, rundown building with a new clothing store is a great idea. I encourage city council to vote in favor of this project.

Some city council members have argued that the old building holds a lot of historic value because it was built before the Civil War. However, they fail to mention that the building has fallen into a state of disrepair. Pieces of broken glass and brick could easily fall to the ground and hurt people on the sidewalk. The building is just not safe.

Replacing the old building with a new store will improve the appearance of the downtown area. Right now, the old building is full of broken windows. The doors are missing and it's home to many bats and rats. More than anything, the building is an eyesore. A new building of any kind would be an improvement.

Finally, the old building is empty and useless. It's taking up a lot of valuable property and not being used for anything. Building a new store in its place would bring more people and more money into the city.

In conclusion, I would like to encourage all city council members to think about how wonderful Main Street could look if an unsafe, useless, eyesore of a building was removed and replaced with a brand new store.

In order to achieve the highest score for your essay, make sure that you use the three stages of writing and the Writer's Checklist. Also, pay attention to the content and organization of your essay, as well as usage, sentence construction, and mechanics.

Content/Organization

As mentioned earlier, your essay should be framed by strong opening and closing ideas. Make sure that you have addressed reasons that your issue is important. Conclude by stating why you feel as you do.

In between the opening and closing of your essay are your main ideas. Make sure that your ideas are clear, and that you have included a variety of main ideas and have not simply stressed the same point multiple times. Your ideas should follow a logical progression, meaning that transition from one main idea to another should not be choppy, but instead should flow easily from one idea to the next. Your ideas should also be supported by details, or reasons why you believe your ideas to be true. Also, be sure that your transitions from the introduction to the body to the conclusion are fluid instead of choppy.

Sentence Construction

Make sure that you follow traditional grammar rules when composing sentences. You should check to make sure that you have placed periods and commas in logical places. Make sure that you vary the length and structure of your sentences. This will help to improve your composition.

Usage

When you revise and edit, make sure that you use correct verb tense and agreement. For example, if you are using past tense verbs to describe something that happened in the past, then make sure that all the verbs describing this past event are in the past tense. Also, look at your pronouns (*I, you, he, she, it, we, they*) to make sure that you have used them correctly. Examine your essay to make sure you have used words that will engage the reader. If you don't like the look or sound of a certain word in your essay, try to replace it with a better one.

Mechanics

Mechanics are the spelling, capitalization, and punctuation in your essay. You are not allowed to use a dictionary during the test, so try to do your best with spelling and capitalization. Using precise spelling, capitalization, and punctuation will make it easier for people to read and understand your essay.

Lesson 2: Writing to Speculate

This lesson covers the skills for writing an essay, in response to a picture prompt, that

- Responds clearly and stays focused on the picture and prompt
- Selects a focus and supports it with details
- Includes an introduction, appropriate transitions, and a conclusion
- Uses a variety of words and details to engage readers
- Uses varied sentence structure and word choice
- Uses conventions of print and literary forms
- Uses language appropriate to the audience
- Is revised and edited for content/organization, usage, sentence contruction, and mechanics
- Combines information from a variety of sources in a written response

On the MCAS, you may be asked to write to speculate. In this case, you will be given a picture prompt and asked to write a story to explain what's happening in the picture. For example, you may be presented with a picture prompt similar to the following:

Every picture tells a story, but the stories we see may be different. Look closely at the picture. What story is it telling? Use your imagination and experience to speculate what the story is about or to describe what is happening.

In order to respond to this question, you must examine the picture carefully. What do you see? Where is the story taking place? Who is in the picture? What stands out about the picture? How does the picture make you feel? What do you think the purpose of this picture might be? As you look at the picture and ask yourself these questions, jot down notes about what you think is happening and organize your ideas. Remember to use the three stages of writing (prewriting, drafting, and revising) as you prepare your story. Also use the Writer's Checklist on page 39.

When you are writing to speculate, remember to pay attention to the content and organization of your essay, as well as word usage, sentence construction, and mechanics (spelling, capitalization, and punctuation). Here is an example of a top-graded response to the prompt provided at the beginning of this lesson.

For months Nancy's friend Susan had begged her to join the Women's Suffrage Association of New Jersey. She told Nancy about all of the wonderful changes women could make, laws they could create, and jobs they could have, if only they had the right to vote. Nancy listened carefully, but she was uncertain about joining the group. Nancy's mother had always told her that women had no place in the government. "Women should stay home, care for the children, and do housework," she had said. Secretly Nancy hated housework, but she kept her opinion quiet to appease her mother.

One day, as Nancy walked down Main Street, she saw a group of men reading posters in the window of the National Association of Men Opposed to Woman Suffrage. The men talked and laughed about the posters.

"The right to vote," chuckled one man. "What next? A woman for president?"

The men snickered.

As Nancy peered over her shoulder, she thought, *A woman president? That's not such a bad idea.* With that thought in her mind, Nancy raced to her friend Susan's house. She knew the suffrage meeting was about to start and she wasn't going to stay silent any more. She wanted to make her voice heard and her vote count.

This story would earn high marks because it shows an excellent command of written language. It is a well-developed story with plenty of detail and distinct focus. The subjects and verbs agree, pronouns are used correctly, and verb tenses are used appropriately. Sentences vary in length and construction, and there are no errors in capitalization, punctuation, and spelling.

Lesson 3: Writing to Analyze/Explain

This lesson covers the following skills for reading and analyzing a poem or text to

- Find a theme or central idea
- Look for details that develop or support the main idea
- Recognize a purpose for reading
- Make judgments, form opinions, and draw conclusions from the text
- Interpret textual conventions and literary elements

and writing an essay, in response to a writing prompt, that:

- Responds clearly and stays focused on the prompt
- Selects a focus and supports it with details
- Includes an introduction, appropriate transitions, and a conclusion
- Uses a variety of words and details to engage readers
- Uses varied sentence structure and word choice
- Uses conventions of print and literary forms
- Uses language appropriate to the audience
- Is revised and edited for content/organization, usage, sentence construction, and mechanics
- Combines information from a variety of sources in a written response

On the MCAS, you might be asked to write to analyze or explain. In this case, you will be asked to read a poem and given a writing prompt related to the poem. The prompts for this type of writing usually give you a statement about the poem and ask you to respond to the statement. Here is an example of the kind of poem and prompt you might see on this part of the test.

My November Guest
by Robert Frost

My sorrow, when she's here with me, *a*
    Thinks these dark days of autumn rain *b*
Are beautiful as days can be; *a*
She loves the bare, the withered tree; *a*
    She walks the sodden pasture lane. *b*

Her pleasure will not let me stay. *a*
    She talks and I am fain to list: *b*
She's glad the birds are gone away, *a*
She's glad her simple worsted gray *a*
    Is silver now with clinging mist. *b*

The desolate, deserted trees, *a*
    The faded earth, the heavy sky, *b*
The beauties she so truly sees, *a*
She thinks I have no eye for these, *a*
    And vexes me for reason why. *b*

Not yesterday I learned to know *a*
    The love of bare November days *b*
Before the coming of the snow, *a*
But it were vain to tell her so, *a*
    And they are better for her praise. *b*

In this poem, the reader learns about the hidden beauties of a cold November day.

- Think about your favorite day, month, or season of the year. Why do you enjoy this time of year so much?

- Write an explanation of your favorite time of year and analyze why it is so special to you.

Include details, facts, and examples to develop your analysis.

In order to respond to this prompt, you must think about the poem you read and your own experiences. What types of things does the author discuss in the poem? What time of year do you enjoy the most? What makes this time of year special? Ask yourself these questions and jot down notes and organize your ideas. Remember to use the three stages of writing (prewriting, drafting, and revising) as you prepare your response. Also use the Writer's Checklist in Part A, Lesson 1.

When writing to analyze or explain, keep in mind that a top-score response has a clear opening and closing and progresses logically from beginning to end. Top-graded responses have few, if any, errors in usage, sentence construction, and mechanics.

The following is an example of a top-graded response to the prompt at the beginning of this lesson.

My favorite season of the year is autumn. [fall] I love all of the changes in nature, the beautiful sights, and the wonderful smells of autumn.

In autumn, the hot, humid summer air turns cool and crisp. The forest behind my house begins to change color. The lush greens of summer become an array of warm autumn hues [shades] like red, orange, brown, and gold. When the sun shines through the trees, it looks like the forest is a great fire trying to warm the gray sky.

As I ride through the countryside, fields are dotted with bright orange pumpkins and shiny red apples hang from trees, ready for picking. At night the temperature drops dramatically and I can see my breath in the air. The smell of wood smoke from the chimneys of neighboring houses fills the air. On my porch, I listen to the sounds of the woods—twigs cracking in the dark blanket of the night forest and a light breeze scraping fallen leaves across the paved driveway. I snuggle deeper into a wool blanket to keep off the chill of a potential frost and sip warm apple cider with my family.

These tastes, sounds, smells, and sights of fall are special to me because I know that winter is on its way. I know that soon my family will be curled up on cozy couches next to a blazing fire. My house will take on new warmth; not the hot, sticky air of summer, but the warmth you feel when you come in from the cold.

This answer clearly responds to the prompt. It has good opening and closing statements and progresses logically from beginning to end. The essay is well-developed and stays focused on the topic throughout. The essay has very few, if any, errors in usage, sentence construction, and mechanics.

Lesson 4: Writing to Persuade

This lesson covers the following skills for writing a persuasive essay that:

- Responds clearly and stays focused on the prompt
- Selects a focus and supports it with details
- Includes an introduction, appropriate transitions, and a conclusion
- Uses a variety of words and details to engage readers
- Uses varied sentence structure and word choice
- Uses conventions of print and literary forms
- Uses language appropriate to the audience
- Is revised and edited for content/organization, usage, sentence construction, and mechanics
- Combines information from a variety of sources in a written response

On the MCAS, you may be asked to write to persuade. You will be presented with an issue that affects your school or community and asked to write a response in support of or against the issue. This type of writing is similar to the example given in Part A, Lesson 1: Writing, but here we work with another example. The persuasive writing prompt on the test may look something like the following:

> At the last school board meeting, the principal asked permission to cancel all field trips for the remainder of the year in an effort to cut school spending. School board members and parents who attended the meeting were divided on the issue. Some people called field trips "vacations" from school and felt they were unnecessary expenses, while others said that field trips give students a valuable opportunity to learn in a different setting.
>
> The school board decided to table the issue until the next meeting so they could obtain feedback from students on this important issue. What is your opinion of school field trips?
>
> Write a letter to the school board explaining your position on this issue. Use facts and examples to develop your argument.

How would you begin to tackle this issue? First, you would decide whether you were in favor of or against eliminating field trips. Do you agree that field trips are unnecessary, or do you think they are an important part of learning? Once you decide your position on the issue, begin writing some notes that support your opinion. Use the three stages of writing (prewriting, drafting, and revising) that you learned in Part A, Lesson 1.

When your draft is finished and you've revised and edited your work, remember to check the Writer's Checklist to make sure you've done everything you can to perfect your essay. Pay attention to content and organization, word usage, sentence construction, and mechanics.

The following is an example of a top-graded response to the writing prompt in this lesson.

Dear School Board:

School field trips should not be canceled for the rest of the school year. I understand how people might mistake a field trip for a mini-vacation from school. Students get to take a break from the monotony of a school day, get on a bus, and travel to a theater, an art museum, a science center, or a historical site. They get to watch plays, see magnificent works of art, try new inventions, or experience life as it was in the past.

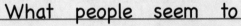
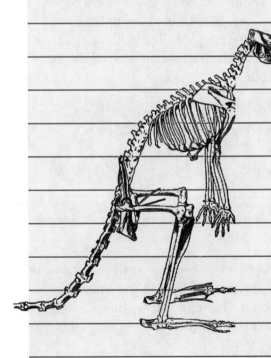

What people seem to forget, however, is that these field trips don't allow us to take a vacation from our education. Rather, field trips allow us to enhance what we've learned in the classroom. While books, chalkboards, and lectures are important, hands-on learning gives students the opportunity to take what they have learned in the classroom and see how it is applied in real life.

Why silently read a play when you can see it performed live? Why study paintings in a book when you can look at them in person? Why study pictures of the parts of a flower when you can visit a greenhouse and study the real thing?

Field trips provide us not only with a break from the monotony of a regular school day, but a chance to supplement what we learn in the classroom. It would be a mistake to take away this important part of our education simply to save money.

Sincerely,

Josh Greene

This answer would earn top marks because it shows superior command of the English language. The author clearly introduces his argument in the first line of the letter. He clearly understands both points of view in this issue and uses the opposing view to make his own argument clear. The essay is well-developed and includes a variety of words. Sentences vary in length and construction, and there are few, if any, errors in spelling, punctuation, and capitalization.

PART B:
Language and Literature

Lesson 1: Recognition of a Central Idea or Theme

This lesson covers the following standards for Grade 7: English Language Arts, Language, and Literature:

- Reading and Literature Strand
  - Standard 8: Understanding a Text
  - Standard 12: Fiction
  - Standard 13: Nonfiction
  - Standard 15: Style and Language

What Is the Central Idea or Theme?

The **central** or **main idea** is the essential message of a passage. Sometimes the central idea is stated in a passage, meaning you can actually put your finger on a sentence or two expressing the central idea. Other times the central idea is not stated and you have to determine it from the information in the passage.

In narrative (fictional) passages, the central idea is called the **theme**. The theme is the overall message or impression the author is trying to convey. You won't be able to put your finger on a theme in a narrative passage. You have to read the passage to determine the theme.

Supporting details explain and expand upon the central idea or theme. They provide more information about the central idea or theme. Supporting details might be facts, examples, or descriptions.

Test questions about the central idea or theme might ask you what the passage is specifically about or what the passage is mainly about. They might also ask you to identify the main idea of a paragraph in the passage. Questions about supporting details may ask you which detail supports the author's main idea. They might also ask you to correctly identify supporting details in a passage. For example, you might be asked, "What causes the children to enter the house?"

 # Activity 1

Read the following paragraph. Think about the main idea, what the whole paragraph is about, as you read. Then fill in the graphic organizer underneath the paragraph.

Ancient Egyptian physicians were very advanced for their time, but some of their "cures" for illnesses and diseases were way off base. While these physicians had some clinical knowledge, meaning they based some of their treatment on science, they were also very superstitious and offered their patients magical cures. If you lived in ancient Egypt and had a stomach ache, your doctor might tell you to crush a hog's tooth and put it inside of a sugar cake and eat it. To cure a headache, your doctor would advise you to fry a catfish skull in oil and rub this oil on your head. If you had trouble with your eyes, your physician would mix together special ingredients, including parts of a pig, put the mixture in your ear, and say, "I have brought this thing and put it in its place. The crocodile is weak and powerless."

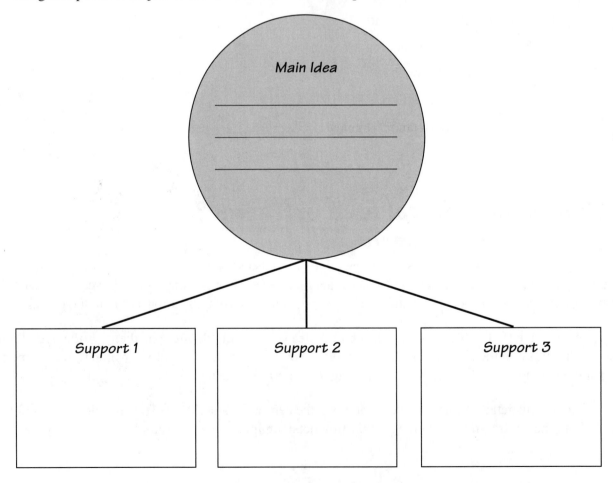

Activity 2

Break into groups of about four or five. Write a paragraph containing supporting details using one of the following sentences as the main idea.

- My summer vacation was really great last year.

- Sometimes you can learn an important lesson from making a big mistake.

- Heroes come in all shapes and sizes.

Passage 1

Now read this passage. Think about the main idea as you read. Then answer the questions that follow.

The Trail of Tears

One of the saddest events in the history of our nation was the forced removal of the Cherokee Indians from their homelands in the southeastern regions of the United States to the Oklahoma Territory in the Midwest. By the time the Cherokee reached Oklahoma, they had lost more than four thousand of their friends, relatives, and loved ones. The thousand-mile trail they left behind them came to be called "*Nunna dual Tsuny*," or "The Trail Where They Cried."

Principal Chief John Ross

In 1776, the United States declared its independence from Great Britain and set about establishing a new nation where all people were considered equal. The founding fathers of the United States drafted the Constitution in 1787 and by 1790 all thirteen of the original colonies had ratified the Constitution. Soon after, the new United States of America began to grow by leaps and bounds. Both population and territories increased. European settlers arrived in America and explored new lands. They pushed further into the frontier, forcing many Native American tribes from their homelands. By 1830, settlers had flooded into Georgia and increased the population of the state several times over. A large number of Cherokee Indians had lived in Georgia for many years before the settlers began to arrive, but their lives were about to change dramatically.

For a while, the settlers and the Cherokee shared the land and resided together peacefully. The Cherokee adapted to the European way of life that the settlers had brought with them to America. They adopted European dress, built roads, schools, and churches, and began raising cattle and farming. Some Cherokee Indians even married white settlers. The discovery of gold on Cherokee lands, however, prompted some settlers to urge the United States government to remove the Cherokee from their homeland. In 1830, the United States Congress passed the Indian Removal Act, which called for Native Americans to be removed from their lands in the east and transferred to lands in the west. The removal of Native American people from their home territories created more space for settlers and allowed them to take control of the valuable resources found on the land. While the removal was good for the settlers, it was devastating for the Native Americans. In 1832, the Cherokee won a small victory when the United States Supreme Court declared the removal laws invalid. The court said that the Cherokee belonged to their own nation and that the only way the United States could remove them from their lands was through a treaty.

By 1835, the Cherokee Nation was divided on removal practices. While the large majority of Cherokee Indians followed Principal Chief John Ross, a small number followed Major John Ridge. Ross wanted to negotiate with Congress. With the backing of the Cherokee council, Ross asked Congress to recognize the Cherokee people as full citizens of the United States with voting rights and representatives in Congress. In exchange for these rights, the Cherokee would agree to give up their land and voluntarily move west. Congress refused to grant the Cherokee these rights, however.

Major Ridge had a different plan for the Cherokee. On December 29, 1835, he assembled a small group of Cherokee leaders, none of whom belonged to the Cherokee council, and signed the Treaty of New Enchota. Even though most of the Cherokee people disagreed with the treaty and fought its passage through Congress, the treaty was passed in 1836 by one vote. It allowed President Andrew Jackson to order the removal of the Cherokee from their lands in the southeastern United States to the Oklahoma Territory.

General Winfield Scott

In May of 1838, General Winfield Scott and seven thousand men began rounding up the Cherokee from their homelands. Within a few weeks, they had captured or killed most of the Cherokee living in Georgia, Tennessee, and Alabama. The soldiers separated families and gave them little time to gather personal belongings and important possessions. Cherokee men, women, and children were gathered in shabby, disease-ridden camps with little shelter and food. Then, the Cherokee began the forced march, more than a thousand miles of rugged terrain and rushing rivers, from Georgia to Oklahoma during the fall and winter of 1838 and 1839.

The first groups of Cherokee to make the devastating journey lost many to disease and illness. John Ross asked General Scott to allow him to lead some of his people to the Oklahoma Territory and Scott agreed. Ross divided the people into smaller groups so they could travel separately and look for food along the way. While Ross managed to spare the lives of many of his people, it is estimated that approximately four thousand Cherokee died along the Trail of Tears. With little time to mourn the death of loved ones, the Cherokee labeled their march "*Nunna dual Tsuny*," or "The Trail Where They Cried." Today this trail is known as the Trail of Tears.

Questions

1. Write a phrase telling what this passage is mostly about.

    _____

2. Now, write a sentence expressing the central idea of this passage.

    _____

    _____

3. Identify three supporting details in the passage.

    _____

    _____

    _____

    Check your answers on the next page. Read the explanation after each answer.

Passage 1: "The Trail of Tears"

 Answers

1. Your answer should contain a phrase, such as "Trail of Tears," or "Cherokee forced to move." (Understanding a Text)

2. Your answer should contain a sentence stating what the passage is about, such as "The passage is mostly about the reasons the Cherokee were forced to move to Oklahoma and the pain they suffered during this move." (Understanding a Text)

3. Remember that supporting details expand upon the main idea. Here are some supporting details, but there are others! (Understanding a Text)

    a. The settlers urged the United States government to remove the Cherokee from their homeland when they discovered gold on the land.

    b. The removal was good for the settlers, but it was terrible for the Cherokee.

    c. When the Cherokee reached Oklahoma, they had lost more than four thousand of their loved ones.

Passage 2

Now read this passage. Think about the central idea as you read. Then answer the questions that follow.

The Ideal Bunkhouse

Alejandro kicked a stone across the sidewalk and sighed downheartedly. "I've had so much to do lately, between chores and schoolwork," he commented. "I'd love to go somewhere peaceful and just kick back and relax."

"Me, too," remarked Jerry. He reached into his pockets and pulled them inside-out. "I don't have enough money to take a vacation, though."

The two friends considered their predicament for a few moments, and then looked at each other and exclaimed in unison: "We'll build a new bunkhouse!"

Alejandro and Jerry had built a bunkhouse several years ago, but that one had been shoddy and un-sophisticated—"very childish," was how Jerry described it. They had used old, knotted wood that they had excavated from a junk pile, and hammered it together clumsily. The roof leaked, one wall collapsed, and the door fell off completely; in short, their first bunkhouse was a disaster. Now that they were older and more knowledgeable, they knew they could do better.

The friends found a vacant yard behind their apartment building that seemed perfect for their new construction project. They consulted Mrs. Fernando, the owner of the land, and she gave them permission to build their bunkhouse there. Now they had a location and permission, and it seemed like no obstacles stood in their way. They raced to the yard, laughing excitedly.

"If we start now, we can finish in a few hours," Jerry concluded enthusiastically.

"No way," Alejandro protested. "Remember how we rushed to build the last bunkhouse and how badly it turned out?" Alejandro suggested dedicating more time to this latest endeavor to make it truly impressive. Jerry considered this idea and then agreed. "Now that that's resolved," said Alejandro, "let's split up and gather the materials we'll need." The two friends separated and rocketed off excitedly in different directions.

Alejandro headed directly to the local public library, where he searched the card catalog for titles on architecture. He gathered a pile of books. Flipping through their pages, he saw photographs and diagrams of some of the most magnificent buildings in the world. Some were museums, some were castles, some were skyscrapers, but they were all fine art to Alejandro's eyes. He wanted to build a massive, beautiful structure that would last for years—and to do that he would need to perform a lot more research.

He began brainstorming and wrote down a long list of topics he'd need to investigate, from plumbing to electricity to local laws. Then he went to work gathering information on each of these topics. Soon he had over a dozen books, and he intended to read every one of them before even starting to build the grandiose vacation resort he was imagining.

Meanwhile, Jerry had gone to the local hardware store, where he began searching for lumber, tools, and other supplies that he thought would be necessary for the project. He found some equipment that he thought would be perfect, but when he saw the prices, he started to feel uncertain. All the equipment he wanted was far too expensive. Jerry looked despairingly into his wallet and found barely enough money to purchase a single piece of lumber. "I'd need a million dollars to buy all the stuff I need here," he muttered. He was only very dejected for a moment, however, because he had a surefire alternative plan.

Jerry raced to his Uncle Jim's house. Just a week ago, Uncle Jim had arranged to have an old garage in his yard demolished. The remains of the garage—huge stacks of rotten wood and rusty nails—were stacked up and waiting to be discarded. Uncle Jim told Jerry he could take whatever he needed, and Jerry did exactly that. He gathered as much as he could carry and ran back to his and Alejandro's meeting place.

When the boys met again, they were surprised by the major disparity between the types of materials they had brought. Alejandro had furnished the project with fifteen library books and a notebook already half-filled with plans and theories. Jerry, on the other hand, had brought a pile of old knotted wood and bent nails. Immediately, the two began to quarrel. Alejandro accused Jerry of being sloppy, and Jerry accused Alejandro of being unrealistic.

"Don't you want to make the best bunkhouse we can?" Alejandro demanded.

"Don't you want to make something instead of reading all day?" Jerry countered.

After they'd argued for nearly an hour, they both started to appreciate the value in one another's ideas. Although Alejandro did have unrealistically high expectations, he was correct when he realized that the boys should do some research before they started to build the bunkhouse. And although Jerry was starting the project in a sloppy, haphazard way, he was correct that they shouldn't do so much planning that they failed to accomplish anything.

When they finished arguing, they devised a plan that satisfied them both. They would do some reading, but they would also put the wood to use. They worked together to construct two benches from the wood, and built a simple canopy to keep the hot sun out. Then they relaxed on the benches and read the library books. There they sat for many pleasant hours, planning the ideal bunkhouse that they would build another day.

 Questions

1. What is this story mostly about?

   A. two boys who build wooden benches
   B. two boys who learn to work together
   C. two boys who live in the same apartment building
   D. two boys who built a bunkhouse several years ago

 Tip

Some answer choices refer to supporting details in the story. While some of these details are true, they do not express the central idea. Choose the one that tells what the entire story is about.

2. "The Ideal Bunkhouse" is specifically about a struggle between

   A. planning and doing.
   B. new and old.
   C. neatness and sloppiness.
   D. boredom and excitement.

 Tip

Think carefully about the theme of this story and how the two boys differ in their approach to building the bunkhouse. Why do they argue?

3.   Where did Alejandro go before meeting Jerry to build the bunkhouse?

A.   to a hardware store
B.   to his uncle's house
C.   to the library
D.   to the bookstore

 Tip

This question asks you about a supporting detail in the passage. Go back and reread the passage. Where does Alejandro go?

4.   What do the boys decide to do at the end of the story? Use details and information from the story to support your answer.

_____

_____

_____

_____

 Tip

This question asks you about supporting details found at the end of the story. Re-read the end of the story. The boys argue, and then they come up with a plan using both of their ideas. What do they do?

Now check your answers on the next page. Read the explanations after each answer.

Passage 2: "The Ideal Bunkhouse"

 Answers

1. B   "The Ideal Bunkhouse" is about two boys working together. Alejandro and Jerry learn to overcome their differences and work toward building a new bunkhouse. Answer choice B is correct. While the other answer choices are true, they are supporting details in the story, and not the central idea. (Fiction)

2. A   The "Ideal Bunkhouse" is about a struggle between planning to do something and actually doing it. Alejandro wants to plan as much as possible before building the bunkhouse and Jerry wants to actually build it. (Fiction)

3. C   This question asks about a supporting detail. Alejandro goes to the library to find books about buildings. (Understanding a Text)

4.   **Sample answer:** At the end of the story, the boys decide to put Jerry's wood to good use. They build benches and sit on them while reading the books Alejandro brought about building a bunkhouse. They agree to stop arguing and work together. (Understanding a Text)

Passage 3

Now read this passage. Think about the central idea as you read. Then answer the questions that follow.

A Real Job

Damen Munez carefully explained his current predicament to his mother: he was in the midst of a financial crisis—in other words, he had no money. He was off school for nearly two weeks for spring break and desperately wanted a temporary job to earn some money to put toward a new bike he had seen in a store window. "Even though I'm extremely responsible and bright," Damen explained and held his hands in front of him dramatically, "I'm only thirteen and no one on Earth will give me a chance."

Gabriella Munez raised her eyebrows at her son and smiled. "What about me?" she asked. "You can work at the office this coming week. We have a huge deadline around the corner and could really use some extra help."

3 Damen could barely contain his excitement upon hearing his mother's words. "You want me . . . to work for you . . . at the office? I would ab-so-lute-ly love that—and you won't be sorry. I will work incredibly hard, I promise, and I will make you proud of me," Damen said.

His mother kissed him on the forehead. "I am already proud of you," she said, "but I think a real job would be a great experience. You can start on Monday."

Damen's mother was a book producer. She ran a small company that wrote and edited textbooks for publishers. Ever since they were little, Damen and his sister, Maria, had spent several hours each day at their mother's office, which had a kitchen in the back with a table where they completed their homework while enjoying a snack. Damen and Maria were fascinated with the many simultaneous projects their mother and her staff worked on and they loved being around creative individuals, hundreds of books, and modern computers and software. Damen had always wanted to work at his mother's company, but he never dreamed it would happen so soon. His mother had just given him a precious gift: a chance to use his outstanding writing skills to earn a paycheck. Damen contemplated his first assignment—he was a math whiz, so he figured he would probably be assigned to write a math textbook. He also loved to write science-fiction stories. Perhaps he would be writing a few of these, too.

When Damen and his mother arrived at the office Monday morning, the staff welcomed him aboard as their new "editorial assistant" and he felt truly honored. He had known most of the editors for many years, but he had never been allowed to work with them before.

Damen's mother explained that Matthew, an editor, needed some help fact-checking a social studies textbook. "I will check in with you before 1:00," she said, "when Grandma will pick you up."

"What?!" Damen scoffed. "Why can't I work the whole day, like you and the other editors?"

Gabriella chuckled. "You will be tired by 1:00, señor just you wait and see," she said.

Matthew politely guided Damen to a table in his office and spread out the materials he would need for his first assignment: a printout of the textbook from the designer, a pen, and a computer with a CD in it. Matthew explained that Damen was to verify each highlighted fact in the textbook on the CD and if it wasn't available on the CD, Damen was to check it online. *This is a piece of cake*, Damen thought—until he saw the number of highlighted facts on each page. "I'm supposed to check every one of these?" he asked Matthew, who just smiled and nodded.

Damen quickly realized that verifying each fact was no easy task. He could verify some information easily on the CD, but other facts, like the dates for major events in Mesopotamia, had to be verified online using only credible university websites, which made his task even more daunting.

After about an hour, Damen asked Matthew if he could take a break and stretch and Matthew agreed that this was a good idea. Damen headed downstairs to the kitchen, where his mother was stirring milk in her coffee. Damen told his mother about his work and asked if there was any way possible he could switch to an assignment requiring writing, but she just grinned. "You have to learn to walk before you can run, Damen," she explained, "and besides, work is just that—work—and you have to learn to do what needs to be done without complaint."

Damen reluctantly returned to his workstation and continued his task. Every so often he would look and up and see the other editors typing quickly, answering phone calls, and walking from office to office with folders and books. He wondered how they managed to complete tedious tasks, like the one he was doing, while still managing to be creative when necessary. He also wondered how they could keep track of so many things at once without losing their sanity. They made their jobs look easy, but Damen was realizing that being an editor was actually very difficult.

When the clock struck one, Damen had a headache, his eyes were blurry, his back ached, he had ink all over his hands, and his stomach was growling. Frustrated, he told Matthew that he had only managed to verify the facts in the first few chapters of the book. "That's good!" exclaimed Matthew. "You're a great help. You can pick up where you left off tomorrow."

When Damen descended the stairs, his mother was waiting for him. "Mom," he said, "I don't think I did so well. I had to fact-check a social studies book and I don't think I got as much done as I should have."

"Did you do a good job?" asked his mother.

Damen explained that he knew the facts he had checked were correct, but that it was very tedious and difficult work.

Mrs. Munez raised her eyebrows. "Ah," she said. "You're not quitting, are you?"

"No!" Damen replied. "I'm just trying to figure out how I can do a better job tomorrow."

Mrs. Munez smiled and told Damen that she was very proud of him. "If I didn't know you and you were hired as an editorial assistant here and had such a positive attitude, I'd be thrilled," she said.

Questions

1. What did Damen learn from working at his mother's office?

   A. Being an editorial assistant is hard work.
   B. His mother's office is not as fun as he once thought.
   C. Fact-checking is not as fun as writing.
   D. Saving up money for a bike takes a long time.

 Tip

This question asks you about the central theme of the story. What is the main thing that Damen learns from working as an editorial assistant at his mother's office?

2. What causes Damen to think he did a bad job?

   A. His mother tells him he is leaving at 1:00.
   B. His mother will not give him a chance to write.
   C. He had to verify many facts online.
   D. He has taken a long time to do his work.

 Tip

This question asks about a supporting detail in the passage. Why does Damen tell his mother he believes he has done a bad job?

3. What does Damen imagine his first assignment will be?

   A. writing a math book
   B. writing a social studies book
   C. fact-checking a social studies book
   D. assisting Matthew with his work

 Tip

This question asks about a supporting detail. Go back and reread the part of the story where Damen thinks about his first assignment.

4.   What does Damen plan to do on his next day of work?

   A.   try harder to do a better job
   B.   use a CD to help him with his work
   C.   ask his mother for a new assignment
   D.   talk to Matthew about his problem

Tip

Reread the end of the story to find this supporting detail.

5.   In paragraph 3, the author uses ellipses (. . .) and spells the word *absolutely* with hyphens (ab-so-lute-ly) in Damen's speech to show that

   A.   Gabriella, his mother, is hard of hearing.
   B.   Damen thinks his mother is crazy.
   C.   Damen is enthused about his mother's suggestion.
   D.   Damen is thinking things over carefully.

Tip

Read Damen's speech out loud.

Check your answers on the next page. Read the explanation after each answer.

Passage 3: "A Real Job"

 Answers

1. A   The major lesson that Damen learns is that being an editorial assistant or an editor is difficult work. At first he thinks his job will be fun, but he then learns that it can be tedious and difficult. (Understanding a Text)

2. D   At the end of the story, Damen tells his mother that he didn't get as much work done as he probably should have. This is the reason he thinks he did a bad job. (Understanding a Text)

3. A   When Damen imagines his first assignment at his mother's office, he thinks he may be writing a math book or a science-fiction story. Answer choice A is the correct answer. (Understanding a Text)

4. A   At the end of the story, Damen tells his mother he is trying to figure out how he can do a better job tomorrow. Answer choice A is the correct answer. (Understanding a Text)

5. C   Damen is very excited about his mother's suggestion. The author writes his reaction that way for emphasis. (Style and Language)

Passage 4

Now read this persuasive passage. Then answer the questions that follow.

D.C. Dish
A Forum for the Nation

LETTER TO THE EDITOR

To the Editor:

I am writing in response to the many letters that have recently been published addressing the controversy over Georgia's new 2003 state flag. The new flag is a welcome and necessary change for Georgians. While it is encouraging to read letters from individuals supporting and praising the flag, it is discouraging that some people still think the design of a new flag was unnecessary and that the 2001 flag was a better representation of Georgia.

As most citizens of the country are probably aware, the flag adopted by Georgia in 1956 was the subject of heated debate for many years. One-third of this old flag was comprised of the state seal, while the other two-thirds of the flag contained the Confederate Battle Flag, which was carried by Confederate soldiers in the Civil War. Georgia's citizens held mixed feelings about this flag, and the debate divided the state for years. Many African American citizens felt that the Confederate symbol on the flag advocated slavery, racial segregation, and White supremacy, and considered the flag to be insulting and prejudiced. Supporters of the flag disputed these claims, stating that the Confederate flag was displayed as a tribute to Confederate soldiers and as a proud symbol of southern history.

Concerns about the prominence of the Confederate flag on the state flag finally prompted then-governor of Georgia, Roy Barnes, to change the state flag in 2001. The 2001 flag contained a large state seal in the middle and a ribbon displaying five different flags that were employed throughout the history of the state and the country, one of which was the questionable flag that was being replaced. Georgians

found themselves in an uproar once again. Those who supported the old flag were outraged that the Confederate symbol appeared to be small and insignificant, while those who objected to the old flag could not understand why the offensive Confederate symbol was still displayed. In a passionate speech to Georgia's citizens, Governor Barnes urged the people of the state to accept the new flag, assuring them that it both represented the unity of Georgia's people and embraced the state's heritage at the same time. The people begged for the right to vote on the new flag, and so began a lengthy and difficult legal process, during which Governor Barnes was voted out of office.

I think that the fight to incorporate the Confederate flag into the new Georgia state flag was invalid and insulting to African American citizens, not only of Georgia, but of the United States in general.

While many argue that the Confederate flag is a tribute to Confederate soldiers, are Americans truly expected to believe that the flag is not a tribute to and representation of the days when Black people in America were not even considered citizens and had no rights or powers?

Georgia's history is rich and interesting, and while the days of the Civil War will never be forgotten or diminished in importance, Georgia's citizens must learn to move forward and embrace the mix of people that currently makes up the state's citizenship, just as the former Confederate-flag-waving states of Alabama and South Carolina have done. Governor Barnes' attempt to encourage citizens to define their shared identity by present standards rather than those of the past was progressive and admirable, and I was shocked and dismayed at the number of people who were unwilling to do so. While it is common to fear change, communities—both large and small—must change in some ways because this is the nature of the world and of life; the more obstinate people are in resisting such change, the more slowly the state, and the country as a whole, will develop. Barnes was not trying to take away Georgia's history or pride, he was trying to replace a symbol of hate and turmoil with a new symbol of unity and peace, one that more accurately represents the evolution of the state and country over the past 130-some years.

Georgian citizens are not prohibited from displaying the Confederate flag in their homes, on their clothing, or on their vehicles. Individual freedom of expression is a right guaranteed by the First Amendment of the U. S. Constitution, and this freedom was not abused during the adoption of a new state flag. The Georgia flag—as any state flag—does not represent individuals, it represents a state, and Georgian lawmakers decided that since the Confederate flag was a symbol that was representative of only a portion of the state's citizens (and offensive to another portion), it should be replaced. I think this was an excellent decision.

The 2001 flag has been replaced with a new flag, one that contains no images or representations of the Confederate flag. While the 2003 flag is neutral and not directly offensive to any one group of people, the intensity and duration of the fight to keep the Confederate flag was discouraging. Just when it seemed that the country had moved leaps and bounds away from hate and discrimination, up popped another reminder that we still have such a long way to go. We need to learn to embrace history while at the same time  progressing toward better ideals and situations. We need to remember the hardships of the past, learn from them, and move forward. Citizens of Georgia and of the United States, let us move forward together, away from hate, away from the pain of history and war, and toward a more accepting and tolerant future. After all, our differences are a large part of what makes America such a wonderful and unique place to live.

Sincerely,

Reginald Furor
Atlanta, Georgia

Questions

1. The letter to the editor is mainly about a controversy between

   A. respect and authority.
   B. past and present.
   C. dreams and reality.
   D. history and freedom.

Tip

Why did some people support the old flag which featured the Confederate Battle Flag?

2. Which detail supports the author's main idea?

   A. The Confederate flag was a tribute to Confederate soldiers.
   B. Many people have written letters about the new Georgia flag.
   C. The Confederate flag is insulting to African American citizens.
   D. Roy Barnes changed the Georgia state flag in 2001.

Tip

To answer this question correctly, choose the supporting detail that best supports how the author feels about the Confederate Battle Flag.

3. The author of this letter expresses his feelings about the Confederate Battle Flag and about the new 2003 Georgia flag.

Give one example of why he supports the 2003 Georgia flag.

_____

Why does he feel this way?

_____

Tip

Go back and reread the article before answering this question.

Check your answers on the next page.

Passage 4: "Letter to the Editor"

 Answers

1. B   The letter is mainly about a struggle between Georgia's past and its present, which vary greatly. The author says that people who support the Confederate flag feel that it is an important part of Georgia's history. Those who don't, feel it is insulting to people today. (Nonfiction)

2. C   Answer choice C best expresses the main idea of the letter. The author stresses that the Confederate flag should not be on Georgia's current flag. Answer choice C best supports this idea. (Understanding a Text)

3.   **Sample answer:** The author supports the 2003 Georgia flag because it is neutral and does not offend anyone. The author thinks this is important because the other flags insulted some people, particularly African Americans. (Understanding a Text)

Lesson 2: Paraphrasing/Retelling and Prediction of Tentative Meaning

This lesson covers the following standards for Grade 7: English Language Arts, Language, and Literature:

- Language Strand
  - Standard 4: Vocabulary and Concept Development
- Reading and Literature Strand
  - Standard 8: Understanding a Text
  - Standard 13: Nonfiction
  - Standard 14: Poetry
  - Standard 15: Style and Language

What Is Paraphrasing/Retelling?

For questions asking you to paraphrase/retell a word or a phrase from a passage, you have to choose the answer choice that is closest in meaning. You should look at the **context**, the way the word or phrase is used in the passage, to help you figure out its meaning. Often the sentence the word is used in will be given to you in the question. Other times, the number of the paragraph the word is used in will be given. For example, a question might ask, "In paragraph 2, <u>division</u> means—"

What Is Prediction of Tentative Meaning?

Questions asking you to predict the tentative meaning will most often cite a phrase or sentence from a passage and ask you to choose the answer choice that best expresses the author's meaning. For example, a question might ask, "In paragraph 2, what does the author mean when she says 'Obviously, a division between parties was inevitable.'" You have to read the passage carefully to answer these types of questions. Sometimes, their meaning isn't literal. The author might be being humorous or sarcastic.

Activity

Try to figure out the meaning of these words from the way they are used in each sentence. Look the words up in a dictionary to check your answers. (Vocabulary Development)

- With seven siblings and twenty-six cousins, Matt had a *plethora* of relatives.

- All that remained of the small boat was some *flotsam* floating on top of the water.

- Shaking her head, Shelley admitted the location of her missing notebook was an unsolvable *conundrum*.

- Under the *tutelage* of my older sister Michelle, I finally learned to swim.

- Nan, Lil, Bob, and Ava are names that are examples of *palindromes*.

Passage 1

Now read this passage. Then answer the questions that follow.

Daffodils
by William Wordsworth

I wander'd lonely as a cloud
That floats on high o'er vales and hills,
When all at once I saw a crowd,
A host, of golden daffodils;
Beside the lake, beneath the trees,
Fluttering and dancing in the breeze.

<u>Continuous</u> as the stars that shine
And twinkle on the Milky Way,
They stretch'd in never-ending line
Along the margin of a bay:
Ten thousand saw I at a glance,
Tossing their heads in sprightly dance.

The waves beside them danced; but they
Out-did the sparkling waves in glee:
A poet could not but be gay,
In such a jocund company:
I gazed—and gazed—but little thought
What wealth the show to me had brought:

For oft, when on my couch I lie
In vacant or in <u>pensive</u> mood,
They flash upon that inward eye
Which is the bliss of solitude;
And then my heart with pleasure fills,
And dances with the daffodils.

 # Questions

1. Read these lines from the poem.

   Ten thousand saw I at a glance,
   Tossing their heads in sprightly dance.

   What does the author mean by this?

   _____

   _____

2. What does the word "continuous" mean in this poem?

   _____

   _____

3. What do you think the word "pensive" means in this poem?

   _____

   _____

4. In the third stanza, why does the poet repeat "gazed" and set it off with dashes?

   _____

   _____

Passage 1: "Daffodils"

 Answers

1. **Sample answer:** The author means that he saw thousands of daffodils blowing in the breeze, which made them look as if they were dancing. (Poetry)

2. **Sample answer:** "Continuous" means "endless and ongoing." The poet is comparing the daffodils to the endless amount of stars in the sky. (Vocabulary Development)

3. **Sample answer:** "Pensive" means "thoughtful." The sentence in which this word is used gives a clue. The author says that when he lies on the couch and feels pensive, his mind wanders to memories of the flowers. (Vocabulary Development)

4. **Sample answer:** Repeating "gazed" and setting it off emphasizes that the poet looked for a long time. It also reinforces the trance-like state the poet was in. (Style and Language)

Passage 2

Now read this passage about the history of golf. Then answer the questions that follow.

The Birth of Golf

Hundreds of years ago, most people relied on the land in order to survive. They would spend many hours every day growing crops, gathering wood, and herding animals. Since they spent their days largely out-of-doors, they were of course surrounded by rocks and sticks. It seems only natural that, when they found a few minutes for recreation, they would create games using this makeshift equipment.

Many historians believe that as far back as the reign of Julius Caesar around 2,000 years ago, people were playing a game that involved striking a round pebble or a ball with a tree branch. However, it wasn't until the Middle Ages that this sort of game became very popular. Around 1400, many countries throughout Europe had adopted variations of this simple pastime. The Dutch and Irish played it on the ice of their frozen lakes and canals. This game, called Shinty or Hurling, resembled modern-day hockey.

Other people of other nationalities played differently, but the most unique version of the game developed in eastern Scotland in the 1400s. Here, as legend has it, bored shepherds took up the club-and-ball pastime as many others before them had. However, the geographic characteristics of the Scottish coast—which included grassy tracks, sand dunes, and, most importantly, rabbit holes—made these shepherds' game very special. The shepherds not only hit the pebbles, but they practiced aiming and swinging in order to send the pebbles far out into the meadows—and into the rabbit holes. Whoever could get the pebble into the rabbit hole with the least amount of swings was the winner. The Scottish shepherds called this pastime "gowf."

Once the idea of adding holes spread throughout Europe, most people modified the games they'd been playing. The game became more popular than ever. Soon, England had "goff," the Netherlands had "kolf," and France and Belgium had their own variations. Royalty and peasants alike wanted to participate in this new sport, which would evolve over generations into what we know today as golf.

The game made an impact immediately. It was immensely popular with the citizens of Scotland, who were so enthusiastic about the game that they devoted much of their time to it. They spent so much time playing sports like golf that they neglected their duty to King James II; specifically, they shrugged off their obligation to train for the military. The enraged king, seeing his military might suffering because of the people's obsession with sticks and pebbles, declared golf illegal in 1457!

Even a royal reproach was not enough to stop the Scottish people from enjoying their sport. They created golf courses, called links, along the sandy seashores of their nation. People flocked to these links day in and day out. The most popular course was named St. Andrews. At its beginning it was just a single small tract of land surrounded by bushes and heather shrubs; as more and more people visited it, it began to grow tremendously. The visiting golfers brought business to the surrounding cities, and suddenly there was a great call for golf clubs, balls, as well as caddies (golfers' assistants). The owners of St. Andrews worked over the next generations to expand their golf course, and today it is the largest golfing complex in Europe. At the time, however, golf was still illegal!

The outlook for the new sport brightened almost 50 years later, when King James IV decided the banned pastime was actually quite entertaining. Not only did he lift the ban, but his interest in the sport—like a celebrity endorsement today—made golf more popular than ever. King James himself began playing golf in 1502; in fact, some believe that he was the first person to officially purchase a full set of golf clubs. The royalty of England and Scotland began teaching foreign rulers how to golf.

The sport took a strong hold in France; however, the heart of golf remained in Scotland. The capitol of the country, Edinburgh, hosted the world's most famous golf course, called Leith. In 1744, the first golfers' organization, the Gentleman Golfers, formed at Leith. They originated the idea of golf tournaments, yearly competitions featuring impressive trophy prizes. Additionally, they devised a set of rules for the game that was widely accepted.

Golf had come a long way since the sticks and stones used in the 1400s. In 1618, a special golf ball was created, made of feathers instead of stone; it was called, understandably, the "Featherie." Featheries were so difficult to make that each one was often more expensive than a club! It was a relief to many golfers when less expensive balls were later mass-produced out of cheaper materials, like rubber. By the 1700s, specially designed clubs and balls were being handcrafted by exclusive shops. The club handles were made mostly from special kinds of wood. Many early clubs also had heads made of wood, though some heads were made of blacksmith-forged iron. Today, most clubs are made entirely of lightweight, super-strong metal.

 # Questions

1.   In the first paragraph, the author says people played games using <u>makeshift equipment</u>. This means that the equipment was

    A.   durable.
    B.   special.
    C.   professional.
    D.   homemade.

 # Tip

Remember that people first played golf with sticks and stones. What kind of equipment is this?

2. In paragraph 5, what does the author mean when he says people "shrugged off their obligation to train for the military"?

    A. They were not sure if they were supposed to train for the military.
    B. They did not bother to train for the military even though they were supposed to.
    C. They played games while they participated in the military.
    D. They were sent away to participate in the military.

 Tip

Go back and reread the paragraph. What were the people doing? What were they supposed to have been doing?

3. In paragraph 7, the author writes, "The outlook for the new sport <u>brightened</u> again almost fifty years later, when King James IV discovered that the banned pastime was actually quite entertaining."

    What is the meaning of <u>brightened</u> in this sentence?

    A. lit up
    B. improved
    C. opened
    D. cheered up

Check your answers on the next page. Read the explanation after each answer choice.

Passage 2: "The Birth of Golf"

 Answers

1. D   The "equipment" was really sticks and stones that the people made into equipment. There-fore, the best answer choice is D. (Vocabulary Development)

2. B   The author means that people were so busy playing golf that they did not train for the military even though they were supposed to. Answer choice B is the best answer. (Nonfiction)

3. B   While all of the answer choices could be definitions of the word "brightened," in this passage "brightened" means "improved." (Vocabulary Development)

Passage 3

Now read this passage about reality television. Then answer the questions that follow.

The "Reality" of Reality Television

The American people have suffered long enough: it's time to put an end to reality television. In recent years, reality television shows have become a staple of many networks' programming schedules and it's easy to see why. Reality television offers a glimpse into the lives of people just like you and me. Rather than watching a scripted television show where a famous actor or actress portrays a normal, ordinary person, we can watch normal, ordinary people receive the star treatment, compete in outrageous contests, and win exorbitant amounts of money. Who wouldn't want to live in a "reality" where you can increase your bank account by a few thousand dollars simply by swimming with a few snakes or parachuting out of a plane?

Reality television does have some advantages over traditional scripted television shows. There seems to be an endless supply of topics from which to choose, and an endless amount of people willing to step up and take on the newest challenge. There's always some new show waiting in the wings, ready to humiliate a new cast of characters and spark the interest of a new group of viewers. From the corporate world to hospital operating tables to boxing rings, it seems that reality television cameras are everywhere, witnessing everything. As long as the cameras catch a few laughs, a few cries, and a few fights, producers can take months of footage and piece together several hours of fast-paced, exciting television. Reality shows take less time, effort, and money to create than scripted television shows. There's usually one big pay-off at the end of the show where the winner gets an amazing prize, instead of five or six actors and actresses who are paid high salaries per episode. Despite these few positive aspects, most reality television shows are littered with problems.

Perhaps the main problem with reality television is best demonstrated through a comparison of actual reality and television reality. In the early days of film, filmmakers created documentaries about real people and events in history. For example, a filmmaker might show how Inuit people living in Alaska hunt for caribou. Another filmmaker might capture the ancient rituals of an African tribe or show the effects of poverty in a Third World country. When these documentaries were shown on television, viewers could see how ordinary people living in the real world are affected by real circumstances. These documentaries served as educational tools by showing the actual reality that some people must face. The difference between this reality and today's reality television shows is that today's shows have lost the concept of "reality." Reality shows that set out to represent real life situations that could affect anyone at any time have morphed into outrageous contests that focus on the extremes people will go to get what they want. Can it be considered "reality" to drop a bunch of strangers on an island with no food

or water and force them to compete for a million dollars? Is it reality to participate in all kinds of crazy tests in order to be crowned the head of a successful corporation? Television reality shows are less about real life and more about the best way to surprise a member of the cast and shock viewers at home.

Today's reality shows no longer offer us a real glimpse into the lives of people and cultures from around the world. We don't get to see how people really live, work, and interact with others. We don't get to hear their innermost thoughts and feelings, or see their ways of life. Instead, most of today's reality television shows offer viewers a cast of characters who live in a tent, on an island, or in some magnificent mansion. These people participate in funny, foolish, or outlandish acts to win money, cars, jobs, modeling contracts, recording contracts, and even future spouses. They will do whatever it takes to have their fifteen minutes of fame. These shows pit friend against friend, husband against wife, and family against family, all in the name of entertainment. But what happens when these shows are over and these people try to return to their normal lives? Is it possible for them to go back to their old lives when their words and actions have been immortalized on the television screen for the whole world to see?

It is a shame that this form of television, which could be used to educate the world about so many important issues, is more often used as an expanded dating game or the road to superstardom. Instead of teaching us about the reality of what it's like to grow up as a minority, reality shows teach us how to put a puzzle together with our toes while wearing a blindfold. Reality shows could focus on important issues that people deal with in real life: finding a job after high school or college; volunteering for a community organization; or learning how to perform a new skill. Instead, most "reality shows" give us a group of people taking time out from their normal, everyday lives to take part in some fantastic scheme created by a television producer. And the last time I checked, that wasn't reality.

Questions

1. In paragraph 1, <u>staple</u> means

    A. fasten.
    B. clip.
    C. necessity.
    D. pin.

Tip

Go back to paragraph 1 and reread the sentence containing the word "staple." What does it mean?

2. What does <u>interact</u> mean in paragraph 4?

    A. communicate

    B. care about

    C. understand

    D. know about

Tip

Go back and reread paragraph 4. The sentence containing the word should give you a clue.

3. What does the author mean in the last paragraph when she says, ". . . reality shows teach us how to put a puzzle together with our toes while wearing a blindfold"?

    A. Reality shows teach us many new and interesting things.

    B. Reality shows teach us about outrageous things.

    C. Reality shows are sometimes hard to understand.

    D. Reality shows are only appreciated by some people.

Tip

Reread the last paragraph. What message is the author trying to convey?

4. Why does the author put "reality" in quotation marks in the title and sometimes in the text?

_____

_____

_____

Check your answers on the next page. Read the explanation after each answer choice.

Passage 3: "The 'Reality' of Reality Television"

 Answers

1. C   In this passage, "staple" means "necessity." Some television networks consider reality shows to be a necessary part of their programming. (Vocabulary Development)

2. A   The sentence that the word "interact" appears in says that "We don't get to see how people really, live, work, and interact . . ." Answer choice A, "communicate," is the best answer choice. (Vocabulary Development)

3. B   The best answer choice is B: Reality shows teach us about outrageous things. The author stresses that reality shows do not teach us about anything useful. (Nonfiction)

4.   **Sample answer:** The author wants to reinforce his point that what is called reality in "reality" TV is not actually the reality we experience in the world outside TV. (Style and Language)

Passage 4

Now read this passage and answer the questions that follow.

From H.G. Wells' *The War of the Worlds*
Book One:
"The Coming of the Martians"

Then came the night of the first falling star. It was seen early in the morning, rushing over Winchester eastward, a line of flame high in the atmosphere. Hundreds must have seen it, and taken it for an ordinary falling star. Albin described it as leaving a greenish streak behind it that glowed for some seconds. Denning, our greatest authority on meteorites, stated that the height of its first appearance was about ninety or one hundred miles. It seemed to him that it fell to earth about one hundred miles east of him.

I was at home at that hour and writing in my study; and although my French windows face towards Ottershaw and the blind was up (for I loved in those days to look up at the night sky), I saw nothing of it. Yet this strangest of all things that ever came to earth from outer space must have fallen while I was sitting there, visible to me had I only looked up as it passed. Some of those who saw its flight say it travelled with a hissing sound. I myself heard nothing of that. Many people in Berkshire, Surrey, and Middlesex must have seen the fall of it, and, at most, have thought that another meteorite had descended. No one seems to have troubled to look for the fallen mass that night.

3 But very early in the morning poor Ogilvy, who had seen the shooting star and who was persuaded that a meteorite lay somewhere on the common between Horsell, Ottershaw, and Woking, rose early with the idea of finding it. Find it he did, soon after dawn, and not far from the sandpits. An enormous hole had been made by the impact of the projectile, and the sand and gravel had been flung violently in every direction over the heath, forming heaps visible a mile and a half away. The heather was on fire eastward, and a thin blue smoke rose against the dawn.

The Thing itself lay almost entirely buried in sand, amidst the scattered splinters of a fir tree it had shivered to fragments in its descent. The uncovered part had the appearance of a huge cylinder, caked over and its outline softened by a thick scaly dun-coloured incrustation. It had a diameter of about thirty yards. He approached the mass, surprised at the size and more so at the shape, since most meteorites are rounded more or less completely. It was, however, still so hot from its flight through the air as to forbid his near approach. A stirring noise within its cylinder he ascribed to the unequal cooling of its surface; for at that time it had not occurred to him that it might be hollow.

He remained standing at the edge of the pit that the Thing had made for itself, staring at its strange appearance, astonished chiefly at its unusual shape and colour, and dimly perceiving even then some evidence of design in its arrival. The early morning was wonderfully still, and the sun, just clearing the pine trees towards Weybridge, was already warm. He did not remember hearing any birds that morning, there was certainly no breeze stirring, and the only sounds were the faint movements from within the cindery cylinder. He was all alone on the common.

Then suddenly he noticed with a start that some of the grey clinker, the ashy incrustation that covered the meteorite, was falling off the circular edge of the end. It was dropping off in flakes and raining down upon the sand. A large piece suddenly came off and fell with a sharp noise that brought his heart into his mouth.

For a minute he scarcely realised what this meant, and, although the heat was excessive, he clambered down into the pit close to the bulk to see the Thing more clearly. He fancied even then that the cooling of the body might account for this, but what disturbed that idea was the fact that the ash was falling only from the end of the cylinder.

And then he perceived that, very slowly, the circular top of the cylinder was rotating on its body. It was such a gradual movement that he discovered it only through noticing that a black mark that had been near him five minutes ago was now at the other side of the circumference. Even then he scarcely understood what this indicated, until he heard a muffled grating sound and saw the black mark jerk forward an inch or so. Then the thing came upon him in a flash. The cylinder was artificial—hollow—with an end that screwed out! Something within the cylinder was unscrewing the top!

"Good heavens!" said Ogilvy. "There's a man in it—men in it! Half roasted to death! Trying to escape!"

At once, with a quick mental leap, he linked the Thing with the flash upon Mars.

The thought of the confined creature was so dreadful to him that he forgot the heat and went forward to the cylinder to help turn. But luckily the dull radiation arrested him before he could burn his hands on the still-glowing metal. At that he stood irresolute for a moment, then turned, scrambled out of the pit, and set off running wildly into Woking. The time then must have been somewhere about six o'clock. He met a waggoner and tried to make him understand, but the tale he told and his appearance were so wild—his hat had fallen off in the pit—that the man simply drove on. He was equally unsuccessful with the potman who was just unlocking the doors of the public-house by Horsell Bridge. The fellow thought he was a lunatic at large and made an unsuccessful attempt to shut him into the taproom. That sobered him a little; and when he saw Henderson, the London journalist, in his garden, he called over the palings and made himself understood.

"Henderson," he called, "you saw that shooting star last night?"

"Well?" said Henderson.

"It's out on Horsell Common now."

"Good Lord!" said Henderson. "Fallen meteorite! That's good."

"But it's something more than a meteorite. It's a cylinder—an artificial cylinder, man! And there's something inside."

Henderson stood up with his spade in his hand.

"What's that?" he said. He was deaf in one ear.

Ogilvy told him all that he had seen. Henderson was a minute or so taking it in. Then he dropped his spade, snatched up his jacket, and came out into the road. The two men hurried back at once to the common, and found the cylinder still lying in the same position. But now the sounds inside had ceased, and a thin circle of bright metal showed between the top and the body of the cylinder. Air was either entering or escaping at the rim with a thin, sizzling sound.

They listened, rapped on the scaly burnt metal with a stick, and, meeting with no response, they both concluded the man or men inside must be insensible or dead.

Of course the two were quite unable to do anything. They shouted consolation and promises, and went off back to the town again to get help. One can imagine them, covered with sand, excited and disordered, running up the little street in the bright sunlight just as the shop folks were taking down their shutters and people were opening their bedroom windows. Henderson went into the railway station at once, in order to telegraph the news to London. The newspaper articles had prepared men's minds for the reception of the idea.

By eight o'clock a number of boys and unemployed men had already started for the common to see the "dead men from Mars." That was the form the story took. I heard of it first from my newspaper boy about a quarter to nine when I went out to get my Daily Chronicle. I was naturally startled, and lost no time in going out and across the Ottershaw Bridge to the sand pits.

I found a little crowd of perhaps twenty people surrounding the huge hole in which the cylinder lay. I have already described the appearance of that colossal bulk, embedded in the ground. The turf and gravel about it seemed charred as if by a sudden explosion. No doubt its impact had caused a flash of fire. Henderson and Ogilvy were not there. I think they perceived that nothing was to be done for the present, and had gone away to breakfast at Henderson's house.

There were four or five boys sitting on the edge of the Pit, with their feet dangling, and amusing themselves—until I stopped them—by throwing stones at the giant mass. After I had spoken to them about it, they began playing at "touch" in and out of the group of bystanders.

Among these were a couple of cyclists, a jobbing gardener I employed sometimes, a girl carrying a baby, Gregg the butcher and his little boy, and two or three loafers and golf caddies who were accustomed to hang about the railway station. There was very little talking. Few of the common people in England had anything but the vaguest astronomical ideas in those days. Most of them were staring quietly at the big table-like end of the cylinder, which was still as Ogilvy and Henderson had left it. I fancy the popular expectation of a heap of charred corpses was disappointed at this inanimate bulk. Some went away while I was there, and other people came. I clambered into the pit and fancied I heard a faint movement under my feet. The top had certainly ceased to rotate.

26   It was only when I got thus close to it that the strangeness of this object was at all evident to me. At the first glance it was really no more exciting than an overturned carriage or a tree blown across the road. Not so much so, indeed. It looked like a rusty gas float. It required a certain amount of scientific education to perceive that the grey scale of the Thing was no common oxide, that the yellowish-white metal that gleamed in the crack between the lid and the cylinder had an unfamiliar hue. "Extra-terrestrial" had no meaning for most of the onlookers.

At that time it was quite clear in my own mind that the Thing had come from the planet Mars, but I judged it improbable that it contained any living creature. I thought the unscrewing might be automatic. In spite of Ogilvy, I still believed that there were men in Mars. My mind ran fancifully on the possibilities of its containing manuscript, on the difficulties in translation that might arise, whether we should find coins and models in it, and so forth. Yet it was a little too large for assurance on this idea. I felt an impatience to see it opened. About eleven, as nothing seemed happening, I walked back, full of such thought, to my home in Maybury. But I found it difficult to get to work upon my abstract investigations.

In the afternoon the appearance of the common had altered very much. The early editions of the evening papers had startled London with enormous headlines:

"A MESSAGE RECEIVED FROM MARS."

"REMARKABLE STORY FROM WOKING,"

and so forth. In addition, Ogilvy's wire to the Astronomical Exchange had roused every observatory in the three kingdoms.

There were half a dozen flies or more from the Woking station standing in the road by the sandpits, a basket-chaise from Chobham, and a rather lordly carriage. Besides that, there was quite a heap of bicycles. In addition, a large number of people must have walked, in spite of the heat of the day, from Woking and Chertsey, so that there was altogether quite a considerable crowd—one or two gaily dressed ladies among the others.

It was glaringly hot, not a cloud in the sky nor a breath of wind, and the only shadow was that of the few scattered pine trees. The burning heather had been extinguished, but the level ground towards Ottershaw was blackened as far as one could see, and still giving off vertical streamers of smoke. An enterprising sweet-stuff dealer in the Chobham Road had sent up his son with a barrow-load of green apples and ginger beer.

Going to the edge of the pit, I found it occupied by a group of about half a dozen men—Henderson, Ogilvy, and a tall, fair-haired man that I afterwards learned was Stent, the Astronomer Royal, with several workmen wielding spades and pickaxes. Stent was giving directions in a clear, high-pitched voice. He was standing on the cylinder, which was now evidently much cooler; his face was crimson and streaming with perspiration, and something seemed to have irritated him.

A large portion of the cylinder had been uncovered, though its lower end was still embedded. As soon as Ogilvy saw me among the staring crowd on the edge of the pit he called to me to come down, and asked me if I would mind going over to see Lord Hilton, the lord of the manor.

The growing crowd, he said, was becoming a serious impediment to their excavations, especially the boys. They wanted a light railing put up, and help to keep the people back. He told me that a faint stirring was occasionally still audible within the case, but that the workmen had failed to unscrew the top, as it afforded no grip to them. The case appeared to be enormously thick, and it was possible that the faint sounds we heard represented a noisy tumult in the interior.

I was very glad to do as he asked, and so become one of the privileged spectators within the contemplated enclosure. I failed to find Lord Hilton at his house, but I was told he was expected from London by the six o'clock train from Waterloo; and as it was then about a quarter past five, I went home, had some tea, and walked up to the station to waylay him.

When I returned to the common the sun was setting. Scattered groups were hurrying from the direction of Woking, and one or two persons were returning. The crowd about the pit had increased, and stood out black against the lemon yellow of the sky—a couple of hundred people, perhaps. There were raised voices, and some sort of struggle appeared to be going on about the pit. Strange imaginings passed through my mind. As I drew nearer I heard Stent's voice:

"Keep back! Keep back!"

A boy came running towards me.

"It's a-movin'," he said to me as he passed; "a-screwin' and a-screwin' out. I don't like it. I'm a-goin' 'ome, I am."

I went on to the crowd. There were really, I should think, two or three hundred people elbowing and jostling one another, the one or two ladies there being by no means the least active.

"He's fallen in the pit!" cried someone.

"Keep back!" said several.

The crowd swayed a little, and I elbowed my way through. Every one seemed greatly excited. I heard a peculiar humming sound from the pit.

"I say!" said Ogilvy; "help keep these idiots back. We don't know what's in the confounded thing, you know!"

I saw a young man, a shop assistant in Woking I believe he was, standing on the cylinder and trying to scramble out of the hole again. The crowd had pushed him in.

The end of the cylinder was being screwed out from within. Nearly two feet of shining screw projected. Somebody blundered against me, and I narrowly missed being pitched onto the top of the screw. I turned, and as I did so the screw must have come out, for the lid of the cylinder fell upon the gravel with a ringing concussion. I stuck my elbow into the person behind me, and turned my head towards the Thing again. For a moment that circular cavity seemed perfectly black. I had the sunset in my eyes.

I think everyone expected to see a man emerge—possibly something a little unlike us terrestrial men, but in all essentials a man. I know I did. But, looking, I presently saw something stirring within the shadow: greyish billowy movements, one above another, and then two luminous disks—like eyes. Then something resembling a little grey snake, about the thickness of a walking stick, coiled up out of the writhing middle, and wriggled in the air towards me—and then another.

A sudden chill came over me. There was a loud shriek from a woman behind. I half turned, keeping my eyes fixed upon the cylinder still, from which other tentacles were now projecting, and began pushing my way back from the edge of the pit. I saw astonishment giving place to horror on the faces of the people about me. I heard inarticulate exclamations on all sides. There was a general movement backwards. I saw the shopman struggling still on the edge of the pit. I found myself alone, and saw the people on the other side of the pit running off, Stent among them. I looked again at the cylinder, and ungovernable terror gripped me. I stood petrified and staring.

A big greyish rounded bulk, the size, perhaps, of a bear, was rising slowly and painfully out of the cylinder. As it bulged up and caught the light, it glistened like wet leather.

Two large dark-coloured eyes were regarding me steadfastly. The mass that framed them, the head of the Thing, was rounded, and had, one might say, a face. There was a mouth under the eyes, the lipless brim of which quivered and panted, and dropped saliva. The whole creature heaved and pulsated convulsively. A lank tentacular appendage gripped the edge of the cylinder, another swayed in the air.

Those who have never seen a living Martian can scarcely imagine the strange horror of its appearance. The peculiar V-shaped mouth with its pointed upper lip, the absence of brow ridges, the absence of a chin beneath the wedgelike lower lip, the incessant quivering of this mouth, the Gorgon groups of tentacles, the tumultuous breathing of the lungs in a strange atmosphere, the evident heaviness and painfulness of movement due to the greater gravitational energy of the earth—above all, the extraordinary intensity of the immense eyes—were at once vital, intense, inhuman, crippled and monstrous. There was something fungoid in the oily brown skin, something in the clumsy deliberation of the tedious movements unspeakably nasty. Even at this first encounter, this first glimpse, I was overcome with disgust and dread.

 Questions

1. What does <u>projectile</u> mean in paragraph 3?

    A. rock
    B. object
    C. hole
    D. creature

 Tip

Go back and reread paragraph 3. What do they think the cylinder is at this point?

2. The narrator says Ogilvy "clambered down into the pit close to the bulk to see the Thing more clearly." What does <u>clambered</u> mean?

    A. walked
    B. pulled
    C. crawled
    D. clenched

 Tip

How would you get down inside of a pit?

3. In paragraph 26, the author writes, "At first glance it was really no more exciting than an over-turned carriage or a tree blown across the road."

What does this mean?

   A. It was very exciting at first.
   B. It was only a little exciting at first.
   C. It looked like an overturned carriage or a tree.
   D. It was a very strange occurrence.

 # Tip

Go back to paragraph 26. Read the sentence after the one above for a clue.

Check your answers with those on the next page. Read the explanation after each answer.

Passage 4: "Excerpt from *The War of the Worlds*"

 Answers

1. B   In this instance, a projectile is a large object. The characters have no clue what it is at this point in the story. Therefore, answer choice B is correct. (Vocabulary Development)

2. C   The only answer choice that fits is answer choice C: the narrator crawled down into the hole. (Vocabulary Development)

3. B   The narrator would probably be a little excited if he saw an overturned carriage or a tree blown across the road. Answer choice B is correct. (Fiction)

Lesson 3: Recognition of Text Organization and Purpose for Reading, Extrapolation of Information/Following Directions

This lesson covers the following standards for Grade 7: English Language Arts, Language, and Literature:

- Language Strand
  - Standard 4: Vocabulary and Concept Development
- Reading and Literature Strand
  - Standard 8: Understanding a Text
  - Standard 12: Fiction
  - Standard 13: Nonfiction
  - Standard 15: Style and Language

What Is Recognition of Text Organization and Purpose?

Authors create pieces of writing for many reasons. They might write a short story to entertain readers or to teach a lesson. They might write an article that gives readers information or teaches them how to do something. Authors sometimes write persuasive articles or letters to convince readers to feel as they do or to persuade them to take a certain action.

Questions asking you to recognize text organization and author's purpose will ask you why authors structured their writing the way that they did. For example, you might be asked why an author included an anecdote (story) in the introduction of a persuasive piece. You might have to decide if a passage is meant to inform, instruct, entertain, or persuade.

How Do You Extrapolate Information?

When you **extrapolate** information, you expand upon what you have read in the passage either to clarify meaning or to incorporate your own personal experiences. For example, this type of question might ask you why a character in a short story acted a certain way. To answer a question like this, you might have to infer or predict why a character acted a certain way based on information in the story.

 ## Activity 1

Determine the author's purpose for each sentence or group of sentences below. Write entertain, inform, teach, or persuade in the left-hand column.

Author's Purpose	Sentence
1.	It rained three inches yesterday.
2.	Everyone should recycle unwanted paper.
3.	Once upon a time, there lived a happy little rabbit named Bounce.
4.	Before you begin cleaning your room, you should get rid of all unnecessary clutter.
5.	The author George Eliot was actually a woman writing under a pen name.

 ## Activity 2

In groups of 4 or 5 students, write a convincing advertisement for "Pearly White Toothpaste." Be sure to use persuasive words.

Passage 1

Read the following passage and answer the questions that follow.

Cutting Class Size

"Falling through the cracks" sounds like a scary prospect—and it is. For thousands of students in America, overcrowding in their schools is making their educational experience more straining and less effective. Promising students are falling through the cracks each day. They get lost in the crowd and never receive the individual attention and stimulation they need to reach their full potential.

Fortunately, there is a solution to this predicament. Reducing class size in America's schools is the best method by which we can eliminate these "cracks" in the educational system. This will be a challenging process, but many leading educators have developed a detailed plan to make it a reality.

Where It Should Start

The process should begin in the country's more troubled schools, in which the students' achievements have been consistently lower than average. These schools require special attention, and, by instituting small class size policies, they will receive it. The initial step would be to deliver adequate funding to these troubled schools, which will allow them to hire more well-qualified teachers and provide additional classroom space for the students. Once there is enough room to breathe, and enough concerned, properly trained teachers, the possibilities for the students are endless!

Classes of fifteen to twenty students would be ideal; that ratio of students per teacher would allow more individual attention for each student. Providing this reduced class size would greatly reduce many of the public's concerns about the United States educational system.

Putting Names on Faces

Students and parents alike have been worried by the sense of namelessness that exists in many modern schools. Under the current system, some students are just faces in a crowded classroom. If they aren't exceptional in an obvious way—such as being especially outgoing, academic, or athletic—they will likely be overlooked by their teachers and made to feel like nobodies. For instance, quiet students, no matter how talented they may be, are automatically at a big disadvantage. This is simply because they're harder to notice in a crowded room.

The namelessness problem is usually not a teacher's fault. Many teachers have to work with over a hundred different students per day, as well as manage troublemakers, do paperwork, and, of course, try their best to teach! It can be difficult to remember a hundred names, never mind any more personal details. And it can be impossible to notice small changes in individual students that might indicate more serious problems.

A reduction in class size could resolve these problems quickly. Teachers would have a much easier time getting to know their students, not just recognizing their faces. If a teacher knows a student's strengths and weaknesses, personality and interests, it will vastly improve that student's academic and personal experience. The teacher will be better able to help him or her, as well as communicate in more effective, meaningful ways.

Less Muss, Less Fuss

For many students, the experience of attending overcrowded classes can be a miserable one. With thirty or more students confined in a small room, problems are inescapable. Even if everyone is cooperating, there will be some noise, confusion, and delays. If a student doesn't understand the material and would benefit from another explanation, he or she might be hesitant to ask the teacher for a recap because the remainder of the class might want to move on.

If everyone isn't cooperating, there can be chaos, like yelling, fighting, cheating—all types of problems. It can make the classroom a stressful, depressing place to be. Students who are willing to follow the lesson are distracted and annoyed by other students. Students who don't want to follow the lesson can't be convinced to do so, because the teachers lack the time or resources to properly deal with them.

Smaller classes would eliminate these problems. With fewer students, there will almost certainly be reduced noise and distraction. A teacher will be able to guide the class much more easily, not having to shout over voices and spend valuable time trying to discipline troublemakers.

Our Best Bet

Of course, there are people opposed to the idea of reducing class sizes in America's schools. These critics mostly point to the problems of funding these significant changes. They are correct in that it would be a costly endeavor, but would it be worth the investment? Some critics have presented the challenge that small class size would not guarantee that the students will improve their performance in school. That may be true, but only because it depends on the students and their cooperation!

However, few could claim that the ideals of the small class size plan are deficient. A policy that allows students more access to instructors, and lets instructors become more familiar with students, promises to have a great positive effect on our nation's schools.

Questions

1. Why do you think the author wrote this passage?

   To help or promote the cause of less students

   in a class

2. According to the article, how will reducing class size help students?

   It would help students do better on grades.
   And it would help teachers get to know students better

3. Read these sentences from the introduction of the passage.

   "Falling through the cracks" sounds like a scary prospect—and it is. For thousands of students in America, overcrowding in their schools is making their educational experience more straining and less effective.

   Based on these sentences, what does the author want to show about children in overcrowded schools?

   these students need attention and they
   need to be attended to.

   Check your answers on the next page.

Passage 1: "Cutting Class Size"

 Answers

1. **Sample answer:** The author wrote "Cutting Class Size" to persuade readers that reducing class size is good for students. (Nonfiction)

2. **Sample answer:** The author believes that reducing class size will help students in several ways. It would help teachers get to know students better, so students are not just nameless faces in a crowd. It would also reduce distractions as well as help teachers and students communicate more effectively. (Understanding a Text)

3. **Sample answer:** The author is trying to show that students who do not receive the attention they need at school are seriously harmed and that many students in American schools today do not receive this attention. (Understanding a Text)

Passage 2

Read this narrative passage. Then answer the questions that follow.

A Costly Lesson

In just three short months, Gabriella would begin high school. She was excited about this important transition and saw it not only as a chance to change schools, but also as a graduation from childhood. Walking around her room, she surveyed her possessions and contemplated her life. Suddenly, she felt disappointed by her slow progression into adulthood. "Look at all these kiddy things," she commented, glowering at the stuffed animals and picture books she had had since she was a toddler. "I need to get rid of all of this and redesign myself."

Over the weekend Gabriella found some boxes and began stacking all her old toys and books in them. It was exciting to see her shelves becoming clear and to imagine all the grownup things she would accumulate in the upcoming years to fill them.

She was so excited, in fact, that she did not pay close attention to what she was doing. Only for one instant did she hesitate, and that was when she paused to look at a worn purple bear she had treasured as a baby. It had little circular paws, whiskers, and an optimistic smile. She had named it Oscar and lugged it with her wherever she roamed. Now Oscar was a bit battered and threadbare from all her affection, which she noticed just before she dropped it into the box. *Maybe the second-hand store could sell old Oscar for fifty cents*, she thought. Since the money would be contributed to charity, it seemed like a great deal all around.

When Gabriella had packed all of her childhood possessions into the boxes, she taped the lids shut and carried them to the drop-off window at the second-hand store. She placed the heavy parcels down with a thud. A worker there thanked her for her donation and then carried the boxes into a storage room. Gabriella strode away feeling refreshed and very mature.

Although her room was almost empty now, she thought it had great potential for becoming a young woman's room and would suit her well now that she was nearly grown up. The shelves were empty except for the dust that had fallen between her outdated, former possessions. She retrieved some towels and mopped up the dust and then sat on her bed as she imagined some of the remarkable new things she could gather and display on the shelf. No ideas came to her immediately, but she figured they would soon enough. Satisfied, she lay back on the bed and fell asleep.

Gabriella awoke during the middle of the night and was unable to fall asleep again. Tonight the moonlight was too bright on her face; normally it was blocked by the stuffed animals on the shelf above her head. Gabriella sat up and examined the shelf, which appeared empty and lifeless. *Oh well*, she thought with a shrug, *at least it's more adult now*. Then she collapsed back down onto the pillows, though she remained too restless to sleep well.

In the morning she was not only exhausted but downhearted and felt as though something was missing. The sensation was so uncomfortable that she just couldn't ignore it. Throughout the afternoon, she wondered if her decision to get rid of her old things had been a good one. Her room definitely looked more mature now, but it also looked barren. Gabriella decided that, just out of curiosity, she would stroll downtown to the second-hand store and see if they had transferred her donations to the sales floor yet.

Upon arrival, she found Oscar already offered for sale. But instead of being heaped into the toy bin with the regular stuffed animals, Oscar was encased in a glass display unit in the front of the store. Staring closely, she was astounded to see that the price of the bear was $40! Confused, she questioned one of the employees, who explained that he had recognized the bear as being from a special series of toys that went out of production years ago. Not many bears like Oscar had been manufactured and those that had were now prized collectors' items. While Oscar was a little battered, he was still valuable property.

The employee continued, "In fact, a collectibles dealer will be arriving later today to buy him. He'll probably end up residing in a display window at a big-city specialty store."

Shocked and dismayed, Gabriella suddenly realized what she had to do. She pulled out the money she had saved to buy grownup things from her wallet and she bought back her old companion, Oscar. When she arrived home, her mother inquired as to her whereabouts.

Gabriella explained, "I learned an important lesson today. Adults don't have to discard everything from their pasts." Then she proudly returned Oscar to his rightful position on her shelf.

 Questions

1. Which adjective would the author use to describe Oscar?

    A. shared
    B. precious
    C. ordinary
    D. general

 Tip

This question asks you to extrapolate information from the passage to choose the adjective that best describes Oscar. Think about how Gabriella feels about Oscar and what she does to get him back.

2. Why did the author write this story?

    A. to convince readers not to give away items from their childhood

    B. to entertain readers with a story about a girl who learns a lesson

    C. to explain why a tattered bear was worth a lot of money

    D. to teach readers a lesson about growing up too quickly

Tip

Think about what the author's purpose was in writing this story. Then eliminate incorrect answer choices.

3. Why does Gabriella want to change her room?

_____

_____

_____

_____

Now check your answers with those on the next page. Read the explanation after each answer.

Passage 2: "A Costly Lesson"

 Answers

1. B   Oscar is important to Gabriella, so much so that she uses her savings to buy him back from the second-hand store. The best answer choice is B, "precious." (Style and Language)

2. B   Since this is a story, its purpose is to entertain. The author does not try to persuade readers, and the article is not informational. While the story does teach a lesson, Gabriella learns the lesson. The author was not really trying to teach readers a lesson. (Fiction)

3.   **Sample answer:** Gabriella wanted to change her room because she was about to begin high school and was no longer a young child. She thinks high school marks the end of her childhood and feels that her room should look more grown-up. This motivates her to get rid of her childhood treasures. (Understanding a Text)

Passage 3

Read the following passage. Then answer the questions that follow.

Space Colonization: Too Big a Risk

Imagine spending your entire life in a space suit hooked up to a machine that gives you the air you need to breathe. Imagine living in temperatures colder than any place on Earth—even Antarctica. Sound like fun? Obviously not. Yet supporters of space colonization are working hard to ensure that people inhabit outer space during our lifetime. This is no longer just a wild science fiction tale. Advances in technology and recent scientific discoveries about places beyond our planet may have actually paved the way for the establishment of the first space colony.

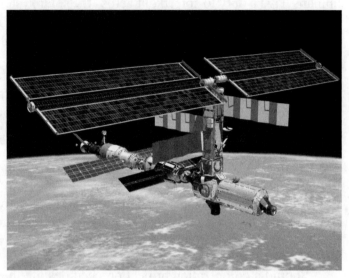

Many people are enthusiastic about this idea, and see it as an entirely positive opportunity for the people of Earth. While supporters of space colonization believe that colonizing another planet would be one of the biggest steps ever taken in human history, they are overlooking the dangers and expenses of such an endeavor.

First of all, the complications of establishing a livable city on another planet are staggering. Even the world's finest scientists are still baffled by the question of how they could keep people safe and healthy on the surface of an alien world. People require very special conditions in order to live, and it would be hard to ensure those conditions on an unexplored new world.

Of all the planets, Mars seems like it would best support human visitors—but it's still an inhospitable place. The atmosphere is so thin it would be impossible to breathe. People would need special equipment in order to get the air they need to live. It's possible that the first colonists would have to spend their entire lives wearing space suits. Also, temperatures on the red planet can become extremely cold, far colder than even the most frigid places on Earth. It might be possible for people to live in such temperatures, but few would find them comfortable.

Although there may have once been flowing water on Mars, today it is a very dry planet. Humans rely on water to live, and colonists would have to bring a large amount of it with them. Special machines would have to be developed in order to recycle the drinking water. Even if the water problem was solved, how would the colonists get food? The Martian ground is rocky and dry; it seems unlikely that any kind of Earth crops could possibly grow there. Until people discovered a way to grow crops, rockets would have to be constantly sent to the colony with fresh supplies. The cost of doing this would be huge.

Additionally, the overall cost of a colonization mission would be downright breathtaking. Scientists have estimated the price tag of a single mission to be about $30 billion. This funding is desperately needed for projects here on our own planet. Social programs of all sorts could benefit greatly from even a fraction of that amount. We humans would be wise to invest more time, money, and effort in improving our own world before we start visiting others.

We must also consider a sad, but important, question: can humans be trusted with a brand new planet? Humans have proven to be very imperfect guests, to say the least. The greatest threats to our current planet are posed by us, its inhabitants. Through weapons, warfare, pollution, and greed, humanity has taken advantage of the natural splendor that Earth once possessed. Some scientists believe that humans have a duty to spread out across the solar system and spread beauty and intelligence. However, over the centuries humans have spread just as much hatred and horror as they've spread beauty and intelligence.

Some supporters of space colonization believe that the nations of Earth would unify and work together to achieve this common goal. These supporters think that all aspects of Earth life, from education to economics, would be improved by the race to colonize space. However, a short survey of history points to the contrary.

History shows that colonization has caused greed, hatred, prejudice, and war among the nations of Earth. Imagine the effects of space colonization! Nations would likely struggle to be first to reach the red planet; then they would struggle for the rights to build on the best land; then they would struggle for resources for their colonists. This could result in further mistrust, fear, and conflict. A Mars colony might end up further dividing the people of Earth and yielding more suffering than discovery.

Should a colonization project proceed despite these many problems, what sort of benefits would it bring to the people of Earth? Some scientists have suggested that we build mines in space to gather valuable metals like iron and gold from asteroids and other celestial bodies. This would return some of the costs of the mission. However, our planet is already well equipped with dozens of types of metal and minerals. In fact, with Earth's natural resources as well as our recycling programs, we have more than enough already. Besides, if we were to build colonies just to make money, greedy competition would no doubt arise that would endanger the whole project.

Some scientists have proclaimed that colonizing the red planet would ensure the survival of the human race. Their argument is that, even if Earth were to die or be destroyed, a group of humans would still exist in their Martian colony. This argument may be true, but it's not convincing because it doesn't apply to our world's current situation. Earth is still a healthy and vital planet and promises to remain that way for a very long time. The human race is growing every year and is definitely not endangered. Generations of humans can live for millions of years longer on Earth—if only we learn to behave more responsibly.

In conclusion, the concept of space colonization is a fascinating one, but it is fraught with problems and dangers. There may be a time when humans are ready to build their cities on the surface of Mars. However, attempting to conquer Mars now, while neglecting Earth, might bring enormous damage to Earth and its inhabitants.

 **Questions**

1. In paragraph 1, why does the author describe what it would be like to live in space?

    A. to prove that humans will one day be able to live in space
    B. to show that some people strongly support humans living in space
    C. to convince readers that living in space would be uncomfortable
    D. to show that humans still have a lot to learn about life in space

 Tip

This question asks you about the organization of the passage. Think about what kind of passage this is and the image the author creates in the first paragraph.

2. Though "Space Colonization: Too Big a Risk" is about one person's thoughts on space colonization, it would be useful background reading for an oral report on

    A. the weather in Antarctica.
    B. what it is like on Mars.
    C. problems on Earth.
    D. how cities are built.

 Tip

Which answer choice is discussed most throughout the article?

3. Which word would the author use to describe people who support space colonization?

    A. uninformed
    B. irresponsible
    C. unskilled
    D. considerate

 Tip

The author feels strongly that humans should not establish a space colony. What does he say about those who support this?

4. Why does the author think it's a bad idea to spend so much money on space colonization?

    A. Not enough is known about space colonization.
    B. We should spend money where it is most needed.
    C. Too many people are afraid to live on other planets.
    D. It might cause resentment among people in other nations.

 Tip

Reread the part of the article where the author discusses the amount of money it would cost for a single mission. Why does he think it's a bad idea to spend so much money on space colonization?

Check your answers on the next page. Read the explanation after each answer.

Passage 3: "Space Colonization: Too Big a Risk"

 Answers

1. C   The author describes what it would be like living in space in paragraph 1 to show how uncomfortable it would be and to convince readers not to support the establishment of a space colony. (Style and Language)

2. B   In addition to space colonization, the author gives information about the planet Mars, such as facts about its temperature, soil, and air. (Nonfiction)

3. B   The author thinks that space colonization is a bad idea because it is unsafe and costs too much money. Therefore, the best answer choice is B, "irresponsible." (Style and Language)

4. B   The author thinks the money spent on space colonization should be used to help people on Earth. Answer choice B is the best answer choice. (Understanding a Text)

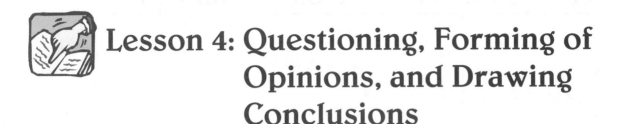

Lesson 4: Questioning, Forming of Opinions, and Drawing Conclusions

This lesson covers the following standards for Grade 7: English Language Arts, Language, and Literature:

- Reading and Literature Strand
  - Standard 8: Understanding a Text
  - Standard 13: Nonfiction
  - Standard 15: Style and Language

How Do You Question, Form Opinions, and Draw Conclusions?

Questions that ask you to question, form opinions, and draw conclusions have one thing in common: you would not be able to look back at a passage and put your finger on the answer. For these questions, you have to use the information and details you have read in the story to come up with the correct answer.

Some questions will ask you to **question** what you have read. These types of questions may ask you to put yourself in the place of a character and predict what you would do in a similar situation.

Questions asking you to **form an opinion** will ask you to reach beyond what you have read and form an opinion about it. For example, you might be asked to identify additional information that would fit in with the story, as in this question: "Ken's older brother and younger sister are able to accept the family's move to Boston, but Ken is distressed with the idea. Give TWO more reasons why a middle-school student might not want to move. Describe how Ken is able to resolve this problem."

Drawing conclusions questions will ask you to decide something based on what you have read. For example, you might be asked why a character performs a certain action or why an author feels the way he or she does about a subject.

Activity

Not everything in print is a reliable source. In groups of four or five, imagine you are writing a biography of a famous person. Select a person, and list some sources that would provide accurate information. Then, list some sources in which the information might not be accurate. Share your group's findings with the class.

Passage 1

Read this advertisement. Then answer the questions that follow.

Center City Science Adventure

Have you ever wondered about the journey of a red blood cell as it gathers oxygen from the lungs and distributes it to other parts of your body? Have you ever thought about how thunderstorms form or how the nitrogen cycle works? If so, the Center City Science Adventure is the perfect place for you to experience science up close and personal.

Since 1997, Center City Science Adventure has established a reputation as an entertaining, educational expedition through the world of science. We pride ourselves on our massive, state-of-the-art replicas of human organ systems, our guided tours to the "center of the Earth," and our magnificent Milky Way Galaxy model. Join us today and experience the wonder and amazement of our bodies, our minds, and our universe!

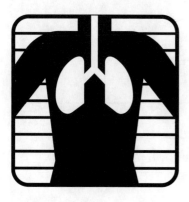

Center City Science Adventure
727 Wright Street
Center City
(555) SCI-ENCE

Take Exit 21A off Interstate 74W.
Turn left at the stop sign and follow
Wright St. to Main Ave.

CHECK OUT OUR EXHILARATING EXHIBITS!

THE HUMAN BODY Tours:	SOLAR SYSTEM Tours:	EARTH SCIENCE Tours:

Circulation Respiration Digestion Muscles and Bones Ears and Eyes	The Nine Planets The Moon The Sun Comets and Asteroids Stars	Under the Sea Earth's Cycles Greenhouse Effect Weather Phenomenon Center of the Earth

Reserve your place on one of our daily excursions through the wonderful world of science. Parties of eight or more, please call to register at least two weeks in advance. **See our special rates for school field trips below.**

CENTER CITY SCIENCE ADVENTURE PRICE GUIDE

3-tour package	$15.00/person
6-tour package	$25.00/person
9-tour package	$35.00/person
2-day pass (all tours)	$50.00/person
Field trip special (5 tours)	**$9.00/child; $12.00/teacher or chaperone**

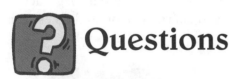 Questions

1. What kind of person would enjoy visiting the Center City Science Center?

_____

_____

_____

2. Would you enjoy visiting the Center City Science Center? Why or why not?

_____

_____

_____

3. Which exhibit do you think is probably the most popular? Why?

_____

_____

_____

Check your answers on the next page.

Passage 1: "Center City Science Adventure"

 Answers

1.   **Sample answer:** A person who enjoys science and wants to learn about the earth, the human body, and outer space would enjoy visiting the Center City Science Adventure. (Understanding a Text)

2.   **Sample answer:** I would definitely enjoy visiting the Center City Science Adventure. The exhibits seem fun and fascinating. (Understanding a Text)

3.   **Sample answer:** I think the space exhibit is probably the most popular because people are fascinated with life on other planets. Most of my friends enjoy learning about the stars and other planets, and I think this exhibit would be the most interesting. (Understanding a Text)

Passage 2

Now read this persuasive passage. Then answer the questions that follow.

"Big Brother" Is Protecting

Dear Residents of Gantersburg:

In 1948, author George Orwell wrote a book about his vision of the future called *1984* in which every thought, every word, and every person were monitored by a powerful ruling party led by "Big Brother." Large telescreens and posters with the words "Big Brother Is Watching You" reminded the citizens of Oceania that they lived under the watchful eye of the government, and that even thinking about rebellion against Big Brother was a crime. While the year 1984 has come and gone, the idea of Big Brother watching our every move is still a hotly debated topic in cities across the United States.

It has recently come to my attention that the government leaders of the fine city of Gantersburg are contemplating the placement of cameras in high-traffic areas of the city, such as public parks, street corners, and sidewalks, to curb the vandalism and crime that have overrun these areas. While I am against Big Brother's cameras invading my privacy and my home life, I urge you to support the city council's proposal. Carefully placed cameras on city streets will help crack down on crime and help police officers identify and remove dangerous criminals from our city's streets.

Cameras have proven a successful tool in decreasing the crime rate in cities across the United States and abroad. In England, more than four million cameras monitor the streets, the banks, the transportation systems, and other areas. It is estimated that there is approximately one camera for every fourteen people, and that the average citizen of England is caught on camera about three hundred times a day. While this may seem extreme, most citizens of England have learned to live with the cameras and know that the main goal is not to spy on the average citizen as he or she walks to work, but rather to identify those people who present a risk to public safety. Cameras placed in public places, such as city streets and public parks, are not used to capture the average person's private, funny, or embarrassing moments on film, but rather to rid those places of muggers, kidnappers, robbers, carjackers, drug dealers, and even murderers. These cameras allow law enforcement officials to see more crimes, respond to crimes more quickly, and sometimes prevent further crimes from being committed. Police officers can identify criminals from the camera images, track them down faster, arrest them, and send them to jail. Some camera systems are even linked to computers that can compare the faces of people on the street to police databases and identify wanted criminals. And as long as you are minding your own business and refrain from engaging in criminal activity, you should have no worries about cameras placed on the street for your protection.

Cameras are already a large part of our daily lives and often times we do not even realize that we're being filmed. Cameras monitor the entrances and exits to many Gantersburg schools, hospitals, and banks. Malls, shopping centers, supermarkets, and convenience stores have cameras to monitor customers who might be shoplifting. Cameras are mounted in and around automated teller machines, or ATMs. Cameras have been installed in several traffic lights throughout Gantersburg to catch people who break the speed limit and run red lights or stop signs. City transportation, including trolleys, buses, and taxicabs, has cameras to monitor riders' activities. Cameras monitor hallways and elevators of apartment buildings and privately owned businesses. Some Gantersburg residents have even installed cameras in their own houses to help boost their home security systems. Whether we like to believe it or not, cameras probably catch more of our daily movements than we realize. What is the harm of a few more cameras placed in high-crime areas to help make our city safer?

The city council's proposal to install cameras on city streets, sidewalks, and public parks does not come without strict regulation. Signs reading "This is a video-monitored area" will be posted in all public places where cameras are present. These signs will forewarn people that cameras are monitoring the area and that illegal activities will be caught on tape and watched by law-enforcement officials. This technology will help police departments make more arrests and stop more crime. These cameras should not be considered Big Brother watching, but rather Big Brother protecting.

Many of you may feel that cameras on city streets are an invasion of privacy, but there is no reason to believe that any kind of privacy exists in a public place. Nothing prevents a photographer from catching a husband and wife kissing in the park. Nothing prevents a newspaper reporter from overhearing a private conversation between two coworkers. When in a public place, we must assume that every action we take can be seen or heard by someone else. The presence of a camera should not make any difference in the way we normally conduct ourselves in public places.

In conclusion, I ask you to extend your support to the city council's proposal to install cameras on our city streets and in our public parks. The only thing these cameras might do is make Gantersburg a better, safer place to live.

Sincerely,

Jonathan Silversmith
Gantersburg, USA

Questions

1. Which of the following contributes MOST to the author's argument in favor of video-camera monitoring?

    A. It may prevent crimes from happening.
    B. People in public are on display anyway.
    C. Cameras are already used in schools and banks.
    D. It will help law-enforcement officials catch criminals.

Tip

If you're not sure of the answer, reread the article. Which point does the author stress the most?

2. The author's feelings toward video camera monitoring are caused mainly by

    A. experience.
    B. fear.
    C. research.
    D. competition.

Tip

Think about why the author thinks video-camera monitoring is a good idea.

3. The author of this passage is in favor of video-camera monitoring in public places.

    - Give TWO additional ways that video-camera monitoring helps people.
    - Describe how you would feel if cameras were installed in your town.

    Use details and information from the article to support your answer.

    _____

    _____

    _____

Tip

Imagine that you were in a downtown area monitored by video cameras. In what situations would this help you?

Check your answers on the next page. Read the explanation after each answer.

Passage 2: "'Big Brother' Is Protecting"

 Answers

1. A Throughout the article, the author stresses that muggings, kidnappings, and other crimes might not happen if people were aware they were being videotaped. Answer choice D is also a good answer, but safety is the author's main concern. Therefore, answer choice A is the best answer. (Understanding a Text)

2. B The author seems to be very afraid of crime and this is his main reason for supporting the installation of video cameras in public places. Therefore, answer choice B is the best answer. (Understanding a Text)

3. **Sample answer:** Video-camera monitoring could also help someone who has become separated from companions, such as a lost child. If the streets were monitored, police would be able to tell parents the location of their missing child. Cameras could also help a citizen who has become lost or injured. Someone would always be watching and available to help. I think video-camera monitoring is a very good idea because it would greatly reduce crime and make people feel much safer when they are in the city. (Understanding a Text)

Passage 3

Now read this informational passage. Then answer the questions that follow.

Arachnid Addresses

Spider webs are a familiar sight because they appear to be everywhere—in houses, in yards, on sign-posts, on porches, and in some unexpected places as well. Most people consider them a nuisance, but did you ever stop to attentively examine a spider web? Each spider web is unique, and some are amazingly intricate. Next time you see a spider web, don't just glance at it—take a closer look!

Why does a spider make a web?

A spider's web is its residence, but it also serves as a snare or trap for beetles, flies, crickets, and other insects, as well as small animals such as birds and bats, which appeal to some large, powerful spiders. Spiders have teeth but they cannot chew, which means that they do not actually devour their prey, but drink the insect's or animal's fluids instead. Not all spiders require a web to capture their prey, such as the ground-hunting wolf spider, which pursues and pounces on its prey, but many spiders do make webs. This is sometimes the only evidence that spiders are present at all.

Different spider species make different webs, and each is capable of producing assorted types of silk. Some spider silk is adhesive and is utilized for catching insects (called capture silk) while some is dry and used mainly to reinforce a web's strength. Different varieties of spider silk are produced and used to bind large prey before it is eaten, compose a secure sac for the spider's eggs, or assist the spider in navigating its way back to its web (called dragline silk). A spider silk strand is elastic and very sturdy when it is stretched out. It begins as a liquid, but just before it is exposed to the air, it hardens and becomes stronger than steel, and because it is so elastic and sticky, it is hard for a spider's prey to break. An insect that flies into a spider web is much more likely to stick to the web than to bounce off or break through the web.

Spider silk, which is actually a protein, is produced in glands inside the spider's body called spinnerets, which weave the silken liquid into a strand that is then released into the wind where it blows onto a surface and sticks. Other spiders will produce a strand and suspend themselves from it, allowing the wind to blow the spider to its next location on the web. Once the spider has attached a sufficient amount of strands on each side, it can run across the web and rapidly move from one side to the other. Each spider web design is complicated, and some take numerous hours to create. The most common types of spider webs are orb webs, funnel webs, sheet webs, and cobwebs.

Orb Webs

The most familiar type of web is called the *orb web*. It is made by spiders such as the golden orb web spider and the garden orb web spider and is recognizable by its wheel shape. Several strands called radii (singular: *radius*) stem from the hub, or center, of the web, and then several strands are laid over each radius in a circular pattern. This process is performed at night and can take several hours, depending on the size of the web. Some orb webs can span nineteen feet in height and six and a half feet in width!

Constructed to catch flying insects, most of the orb web is made from sticky spider silk. When an insect is caught in the adhesive strands, it becomes entangled and struggles to get free, creating vibrations that alert the spider—who often resides in the hub—that it has caught prey. Some spiders, such as the golden orb web spider, can spin a web strong enough to catch a small bird, which often demolishes the web in an effort to break free. Most spiders are too small to eat a meal so substantial, so to prevent damage to their webs, spiders frequently leave a trail of dead insects along the web so that birds and other animals will notice the web and evade it. Other spiders, however, devour large meals and will endeavor to bind the bird with silk threads so that it cannot flee. If a web is damaged in the struggle, the orb weaver spider often deconstructs the old web, regains its energy on a nearby bush or tree during the day, and then rises at nighttime to build a fresh web.

Funnel Webs

The funnel web is a horizontal web, meaning it lays flat instead of extending from top to bottom. Spiders such as the Sydney funnel-web spider, found mainly in Australia, usually make funnel webs in moist, sheltered places, such as under a rock or fallen tree. Underneath the flat sheet of web is a sequence of funnels, or tunnels, that lead to a hole where the spider is concealed. When an insect strolls out onto the web's smooth surface, the spider senses the vibrations, instantly emerges from the hole, bites the insect, and drags its meal back into the hole through the tunnels. Sometimes funnel-web spiders hunt on the surface of the web at night, but most often they stay in the funnel because this is the best place to remain hidden from prey. Funnel webs are very durable, and spiders that construct them often build on them for years. If you see a giant funnel web, you can be certain that the spider inside has been around for a while.

Sheet Webs

Sheet webs are made of a perplexing maze of threads that do not appear to follow a pattern, but they are very large and effective. From above, sheet webs resemble funnel webs, but they do not have a sequence of tunnels beneath. They extend between blades of grass, plants, or trees, depending on the size of the spider. The sheet web spider also constructs a net of threads above the web, so that flying insects are stopped by the barrier and will fall, stunned, onto the sheet. The spider, which waits below the sheet, then pulls the insect down through the sheet, and when the spider is finished

feasting, it repairs the damage to the sheet, which is why sheet webs can last for a long time. Some spiders, such as the poisonous black house spider, create sheets that are several layers thick.

Cobwebs

The cobweb has an even more irregular design than the sheet web. Cobwebs can often be seen in ceiling corners, but they can also be constructed on bushes and the sides of houses and barns. Like the sheet web weavers, cobweb weavers sometimes build a net above their webs to catch flying insects while the spider waits nearby or behind the web. The spider then sprints out, binds its victim, and feasts. Many house spiders make cobwebs, but the famous and deadly black widow spider is also a cobweb weaver. Not all spiders are dangerous, but if you see a black widow, stay away!

Other Uses for Spider Silk

Spiders are not the only creatures to utilize their strong silk—humans have discovered many potential uses for spider webs, too! Some island peoples compose sticky nets from the webs of golden orb web spiders in order to lure and trap fish, while others have even used spider webs as first aid devices to cover fresh wounds like bandages. Spider silk is so sturdy that some scientists believe it may be able to stop bullets—if it could exist in such great quantities. But spiders cannot be farmed, as regular silkworms are, to produce such large amounts of silk because spiders become cannibals—instead of silk-producers—when they are kept captive within a close distance of one another. Keeping each spider in a separate container would be very expensive and difficult, and because most spiders are small, it would not be easy for scientists to collect the large amounts of silk that would be necessary to create the products they desire.

As a substitute for spider farming, many scientists are hard at work attempting to create a man-made form of spider silk. To do this, it is necessary for scientists to clone the spider genes responsible for producing liquid silk. Once they have formed the genetically altered proteins, scientists have injected the proteins into living organisms such as bacteria, into different types of plants, and even into goat's milk, in the hope that one will be able to produce the silk in a similar manner to the way it is formed inside of a spider's body. Then, once a host for the liquid silk is discovered, scientists will still have to figure out how to weave the liquid into a solid silk strand, since plants and other hosts do not have spinnerets!

If scientists are successful, just think of all of the possible uses for spider silk—clothing, bullet-proof vests and other military gear, seatbelts, and parachutes, to name a few. Scientists think that spider silk may even have medical uses, such as in the replacement of ligaments and tendons in the human body. Whether used for webs or warfare, it is clear that spider silk is an incredible substance.

 Questions

1. How does the author feel about spiders?

    A. terrified
    B. indifferent
    C. fascinated
    D. angry

 Tip

Think about the tone of this article. Then eliminate incorrect answer choices.

2. What type of spider would you most likely find in an attic?

    A. orb web spider
    B. funnel-web spider
    C. ground-hunting wolf spider
    D. house spider

 Tip

Go back and read about each of these spiders before drawing your conclusion.

3. The article says that scientists are hard at work trying to create a manmade form of spider silk.

    • Describe some possible uses for this silk according to the article.
    • Give TWO additional uses for spider silk.

    Use details and information from the article to support your answer.

    _____

    _____

    _____

    Check your answers on the next page. Read the explanation after each answer.

Passage 3: "Arachnid Addresses"

 Answers

1.　C　The author seems to be very intrigued by spiders. The author does not indicate fear, anger, or indifference toward spiders. Therefore, answer choice C is the best answer choice. (Style and Language)

2.　D　The article says that house spiders make cobwebs, which are often seen in ceiling corners. Therefore, this is the best answer choice. (Understanding a Text)

3.　　**Sample answer:** The article says that scientists would like to use spider silk to make strong clothing, bulletproof vests, military gear, seatbelts, and parachutes. Spider silk might also have medical uses. Since spider silk is very strong, it might be able to be used to make strong window screens and sails on ships. (Nonfiction)

Passage 4

Now read this informational passage. Then answer the questions that follow.

The Emerald Isle

Known for its rolling green landscape, rainy climate, and rich history, there is an island about the size of West Virginia that sits in the Atlantic Ocean and is often referred to as the "Emerald Isle." Its borders also touch the Celtic Sea and the Irish Sea, and its capital is Dublin. This island is the country called Ireland.

The island of Ireland is separated into two parts. The southern part of the country is called the Republic of Ireland, and the northern part is suitably referred to as Northern Ireland. Northern Ireland is part of the United Kingdom, a group of countries on another nearby island, including England, Scotland, and Wales, as well as a few smaller islands. While Northern Ireland is governed under British laws, the Republic of Ireland, the southern part of the island, is independent.

Much of Ireland's coast is lined with low mountains, while the middle of the island is a combination of flat plains and rolling wetlands. Ireland's landscapes have been the focus of many paintings and poems. Because water-laden coastal winds cause the weather to be very rainy all year, the country is famous for its wetlands, called bogs, where many different plants grow in rich shades of green, including many different types of clovers. According to ancient Irish history, finding a four-leaf clover hidden among the regular three-leafed variety is said to be lucky. The Irish countryside, which includes farmlands as well as bogs, is often enclosed in a dense white fog.

The earliest Irish were primarily farmers, who struggled to produce enough food to feed their families and pay farmland rent to their British landlords. Around the year 1600, the potato crop was introduced to Irish farmers, who instantly loved the potato because it thrived in many different conditions and could feed many, many people. The potato became the most widespread food in Ireland, and its abundance enabled the population to grow. Then, in 1845, a deadly fungus spread through most of Ireland's potato crops, causing them to rot and turn black. The Irish people lost their main

source of food, and the famine continued for years, causing many people to die of starvation. Some tried to eat different types of plants and grasses, while others left the country and made new lives in Canada and America, causing Ireland's population to drop drastically.

Today, Ireland has developed a healthy population of around four million. The Irish diet now includes more than just the potato, though spuds are still a popular part of many meals. Ireland is known for its stews and other dishes made from beef, lamb, and pork, often accompanied by cabbage, onions, carrots, and thick breads. Most Irish foods are warm, comforting, and perfect to eat on wet and chilly days. The Irish also pass time on rainy days with music, often played on the traditional harp, fiddle, and bagpipes, as well as dances, including the Irish jig, which has an interesting history. When Ireland fell under British rule, the British outlawed everything traditionally Irish and imposed British customs—including music and dance—on the Irish people. This meant that performing dances to Irish music was illegal. Some bagpipers were even arrested! The Irish cherished their own music and dances, and so they began to perform them in secret. Irish dance masters  traveled around the countryside, residing with different families and teaching their dances to many Irish citizens so that the dances would not be forgotten. They danced the jig in farm fields, on roads, at secret schools, and even in kitchens on tabletops. They invented new dance steps and sometimes participated in secret dance competitions, where the dance master who knew the most steps would win. Sometimes a dancer's skill was tested when he was asked to perform on top of a wobbly barrel. Now the jig is performed in many different public places, and anyone can learn the steps to this famous dance.

Ireland is also known for its castles, many of which can be found in Dublin, the country's capital city. Ireland's castles are impressively large and have existed for hundreds of years. Citizens and tourists can walk through their magnificent gardens and explore the majestic castles, many of which still have furniture and other antique items belonging to their former residents. The Dublin Castle was built in the early 1200s and was home to many British leaders until as recently as 1922. The Malahide Castle, located on the seaside, is even older than the Dublin Castle and was home to members of the same family for almost 800 years. Other historic buildings in the capital city include large government buildings, an ancient prison that is no longer used, churches (called abbeys), and former homes of famous Irish writers and other artists.

Another immediate association with Ireland is the country's national holiday, Saint Patrick's Day. Saint Patrick was born around the year 385 CE, and at this time, the Irish were a pagan people, meaning that they didn't belong to an established religion such as Christianity, Judaism, or Islam. Saint Patrick was a pagan until he reached the age of sixteen when he decided to become a Christian. He then became a bishop and set out to spread Christianity throughout Ireland, building churches and schools where the religion could be taught. He spread Christianity for thirty years before his death, and two hundred years after he started, most of Ireland was Christian. A famous story of Irish folklore tells how Saint Patrick gave a sermon from a hillside and drove all the snakes from Ireland, which is intended to explain why no snakes exist in Ireland today. While snakes probably never lived in Ireland, the story represents the banishment of paganism from the country.

Saint Patrick's Day is celebrated on March 17th because it is said that this was the date of Saint Patrick's death. While it is Ireland's national holiday, Saint Patrick's Day is also celebrated in America, Canada, Australia, Russia, Japan, and other places around the world. The Irish holiday was once solely one of religious worship, but has expanded to include festivities such as parades, fireworks, concerts, and much more. Interestingly enough, it is said that the first Saint Patrick's Day parade took place in 1700s America, when Irish soldiers marched through New York City in celebration of the patron saint of Ireland. Today, the holiday is very popular in America as well as Ireland.

 Questions

1. Which experience would BEST help you learn about Ireland?

   A. going to a St. Patrick's Day parade
   B. talking to a relative from Ireland
   C. learning how to do the Irish jig
   D. reading an Irish cookbook

 Tip

Select the answer choice that would help you learn many different things about Ireland, instead of only one aspect.

2. Which of the following contributed MOST to the population growth in Ireland after the potato famine?

   A. refusing to rent from British landlords
   B. learning more about the weather
   C. learning how to grow different kinds of food
   D. leaving the country to search for food

 Tip

Read the paragraph after the paragraph that discusses the famine. What does the author say about the Irish diet?

3. The author of the article informs readers about many different aspects of Ireland.

   • If you were to travel to Ireland, what do you think you would like most?
   • What part of Irish culture would you like to learn more about?

   Use details and information from the story in your answer.

   _____

   _____

   _____

Check your answers on the next page. Read the explanation after each answer.

Passage 4: "The Emerald Isle"

 **Answers**

1. B   Talking to a relative from Ireland would probably be the best way to learn more about Ireland. The other answer choices focus on only one aspect of Ireland, such as dancing or food. (Nonfiction)

2. C   The author says that after the famine, the Irish diet expanded to include foods other than potatoes. Therefore, answer choice C is the best answer. (Understanding a Text)

3.   **Sample answer:** If I were to travel to Ireland I think I would appreciate the scenery the most. The article says that it rains often in Ireland and the landscape is a lush green. I think this would be beautiful. I would like to learn more about the castles in Ireland. They sound as if they're very beautiful and an important part of Ireland's history. (Nonfiction)

Lesson 5: Interpretation of Textual Conventions and Literary Elements

This lesson covers the following standards for Grade 7: English Language Arts, Language, and Literature:

- Reading and Literature Strand
  - Standard 8: Understanding a Text
  - Standard 12: Fiction
  - Standard 15: Style and Language
  - Standard 16: Myth, Traditional Literature, and Classical Literature

How Do You Interpret Textual Conventions and Literary Elements?

Several different types of test questions relate to literature. Questions about narrative (fictional) passages might ask you to identify the conflict or the tone of a short story. They might ask about the setting of literature. They might also ask you about characters' motivations, or why the characters do the things that they do.

Questions assessing this skill might also ask you to identify or analyze writing conventions (how the author uses writing to convey meaning). For example, a question might ask you why an author repeats a certain idea or why an author uses a specific technique, such as flashback.

Activity

Read the following fable. Then write a brief character sketch of the fox. Consider what he is like and why he acts the way that he does. (Myth)

The Fox and the Stork
(adapted from Aesop's Fables)

Once upon a time, a fox and a stork were friends. The fox invited the stork to dinner. The fox loved soup, so he placed soup in two shallow bowls on the table. The fox ate his soup, but the stork could not eat hers. She tried and tried, but could not get the soup out of the shallow bowl with her long, pointed beak. At first, the stork tried to be polite to the fox, just in case he did not realize his error. However, the stork eventually became very hungry, and then became angry. "I'm sorry the soup is not to your liking," the fox said.

"Oh, do not apologize," said the stork. "I hope you will return this visit and dine with me soon."

So the two chose a day and the fox visited the stork for dinner. The stork also served delicious soup, but she served it in two long-necked jars with narrow mouths. The fox could not get the soup out of the jar, while the stork had no problem doing so. "I will not apologize for dinner," said the stork. "One bad turn deserves another."

_____

_____

_____

_____

Passage 1

Read the following passage and answer the questions that follow.

Bitter Competition

Sarah Kowalski and Rosa Lee had been best friends since they were very young. They grew up in the same neighborhood, played in the same playgrounds, and attended the same school. However, there was a unique component to their friendship—they found themselves constantly in competition.

For a while, the competitiveness enhanced their friendship. They enjoyed playing chess to determine which of them could outsmart and outmaneuver the other. Whenever they participated in sports, they played on opposing teams in order to determine who could pitch, catch, or throw with the greatest skill. In the classroom they routinely compared their test scores and strived to outdo one another every time a math or science test rolled around.

The Lee and Kowalski families were pleased because the competition appeared to make their daughters thrive. Both girls were honor-roll students who excelled in athletics. What the families failed to comprehend was that both Sarah and Rosa often got frustrated by their inability to get an upper hand in their contests and that this frustration was beginning to take its toll on their friendship.

One morning, the girls discovered that there was an important midterm exam approaching in their Algebra I class. Sarah was distressed about that because algebra was her weak spot. She just couldn't grasp the concept of replacing numbers with letters. Worst of all, she knew that Rosa was proficient at algebra and might take an overwhelming lead in their contests. Sarah was determined to put an end to Rosa's winning streak.

Sarah began studying diligently for the algebra exam a week in advance. Although she felt resolved, she was still having difficulty with the material and the extra pressure of the competition was driving her crazy. The night before the exam, Sarah disappeared into her room to try to memorize all she could. She recited, "The FOIL method—multiply the First term, then the Outer, then the Inner, then the Last. First, Outer, Inner, Last—that spells FOIL." Then she closed the book and recited it from memory. She was thrilled that she had absorbed some information, and thought maybe her cause wasn't so hopeless after all.

The next morning, Sarah watched anxiously as her algebra teacher passed out the exam. She wanted to get the paper in her hands as soon as possible. Otherwise, she feared, she would forget what she had memorized. As soon as the exam was on her desk, she hunched over it and began scanning it—most of the questions dealt with the FOIL method, as she had anticipated. As soon as she began to write, though, her mind went blank. She couldn't recollect what the letters in FOIL represented.

Sarah tried to stay relaxed, but then she glanced over at Rosa, who was jotting down numbers and equations rapidly. Rosa was flying through the exam! Seeing this made Sarah even more uncomfortable and made her memory even worse. Did the F in FOIL stand for "front," "fraction," "first," "furthest"—or "failure"?

Before she knew it, the class was over and she had no alternative but to submit the exam with only a few questions answered. The next day she was disappointed, but not surprised, to see that she had failed the exam miserably. After class, Rosa approached her, smiling broadly. "I got a 97 on that one. What a piece of cake!"

Suddenly Sarah felt furious, and vented her frustration on Rosa. "So what? Big deal—you're better at math than I am and you got a better grade. Well, who cares?"

Rosa was speechless.

"I got a 46," Sarah announced. "And it's partially your fault. I was looking at you writing so quickly and I was so worried about our stupid competitions that I couldn't even remember what FOIL stands for."

Rosa's eyes filled with tears. "Sarah, I'm really sorry," she said, suddenly awakening to the realization that she and Sarah were now more competitors than friends. "I feel awful about your grade, really I do. I'm certain we could work this problem out if we discuss it maturely." Despite Rosa's plea, Sarah spun around and stormed away.

Later in the day, Rosa approached Sarah again. "Sarah, please forgive me. I'm sorry I didn't see how upset you were. You're my best friend—I don't know what I would do without you," she pleaded.

Sarah smiled, though it was a dejected smile. It seemed that she had redirected her anger at herself. "It's okay, Rosa," she said. "Don't worry about it. I'm just a really poor student, and you're better than me, that's all."

"No, I'm not!" Rosa countered. "You just messed up this one time. How about we study for the next test together? This way we'll both be winners—and no more contests. If I lose your friendship, I will be the biggest loser ever!"

Sarah hugged Rosa and accepted Rosa's offer to study together. They promised that from now on they would help each other instead of competing against each other.

Questions

1. Why does Sarah fail her algebra test?

    _____

    _____

2. What is the conflict in the story?

    _____

    _____

3. How does Sarah and Rosa's friendship change throughout the story?

    _____

    _____

    _____

    _____

    Check your answers on the next page.

Passage 1: "Bitter Competition"

 Answers

1. **Sample answer:** Sarah fails her algebra test because she becomes so nervous that, when she sees Rosa quickly completing the test, she can't remember what FOIL stands for. (Fiction)

2. **Sample answer:** The conflict in the story occurs when Sarah lashes out at Rosa and no longer wants to be her friend. The competition between the girls had gotten out of hand by this point in the story. (Understanding a Text)

3. **Sample answer:** In the beginning of the story, the girls are friends but they are also in competition with each other regarding school and sports. After Sarah fails her test and Rosa feels badly, they decide to stop competing and help each other. They are no longer competitors, just friends. (Understanding a Text)

Passage 2

Read the following passage and answer the questions that follow.

A Day to Remember

Charissa brushed her long brown hair and inspected her reflection in the mirror perched on her bureau. The night before, she had stared into her closet for hours, sifting through piles of clothing, searching for the perfect outfit for the special event. She finally decided on a new khaki skirt, a chocolate brown sweater, and a new pair of boots, and she positioned everything on the overstuffed armchair in the corner of her room so her clothing would remain wrinkle-free. After all, not every day was her fourteenth birthday, and Charissa wanted to make sure it was a memorable occasion—a day that she would cherish forever.

When she heard a knock on her bedroom door, Charissa readied herself for her family's traditional birthday serenade—an off-key version of "Happy Birthday," including a colorfully frosted cupcake and burning candle. Charissa opened the door slowly and cracked a slightly embarrassed smile, but to her dismay, she saw only her mother standing outside of her door, holding a basket of clean, unfolded laundry instead of a birthday cupcake covered in frosting and dotted with sprinkles.

"Sorry, dear, but I need an empty clothesbasket," she chirped as she hurriedly dumped the laundry on Charissa's bed and turned toward the stairs, stopping to give Charissa a quick peck on the cheek. "You have five minutes before I officially close the kitchen, so you better hurry and get some breakfast," she bellowed as she descended the stairs.

Charissa's disbelief that her mother had forgotten her fourteenth birthday slowly washed over her, and she lingered in her room until she had accepted the depressing fact. She miserably grabbed her backpack and purse and trudged to the kitchen, following the aroma of burnt toast and strong coffee that was filtering down the hallway. In the kitchen, Charissa's mother was at the counter busily wrapping peanut butter-and-jelly sandwiches in plastic and packing lunchboxes with carrot sticks and juice boxes. Charissa's father barely glanced up from the newspaper as he mumbled a muffled greeting into his coffee cup. Charissa's younger brother, Nicky, sat on a stool at the counter, gleefully spinning himself in circles while his cereal sat, soggy and untouched, in a bear-shaped bowl. No one mentioned her birthday or commented on her special outfit or her perfect birthday hairdo. In fact, they barely noticed that she had entered the room.

Charissa glanced out the window and caught a glimpse of the school bus rounding the corner, so she swiftly donned her thick wool jacket, grabbed her lunchbox and an orange from a bowl on the table, and disappeared out the door, barely muttering a good-bye to her parents. While she considered it despicable that her family had forgotten her birthday, she knew her friends would remember, and at least this would brighten her day.

When Charissa stepped off the bus in front of her school, she was pleased to see that her friends had already arrived. They stood in a small huddle, talking and laughing as Charissa approached, their breath creating puffs of steam in the frosty December air. "Hey, Charissa, did you study for the history exam today?" asked Melinda, frantically flipping through several pages of crumpled, messy notes. "I can't seem to find my notes on the Articles of Confederation."

Charissa reached into her neatly organized backpack for her blue history binder while her friends continued to chatter about some television show they had watched the previous night. Charissa handed the notebook to Melinda, who quickly flipped to the pages she needed. Charissa's friend Polly looked at her curiously. *Oh, this is it*, thought Charissa, *someone's finally going to ask me if I feel more mature, more grown-up, and more special now that I'm fourteen.* However, instead of questioning Charissa, Polly quickly responded to a comment from someone else in the group. Charissa grumbled something to her friends about class and jetted off to conceal her obvious disappointment. First her family, and then her best friends, had forgotten her fourteenth birthday—it was turning out to be the most horrible birthday ever!

Throughout the day, Charissa continually expected to hear the words "Happy Birthday" from anyone—friends, classmates, teachers, the principal, even the cafeteria workers, but no one seemed to remember. By the afternoon, her depression affected her concentration and she was incapable of focusing on Ms. Washington's science lecture about the atmosphere. On the bus ride home, Charissa blinked back tears as she thought of all the people who were supposed to care about her—the very same people who had forgotten this important day.

When the bus arrived at Charissa's house, she gathered her belongings and began the long trek up her driveway. As she ascended the front steps to her house her mother came out on the porch to meet her. Charissa looked at her with tear-filled eyes and her mother gently put her arm around Charissa's shoulders.

"Charissa, I want to apologize," she said quietly as they planted themselves on the frigid concrete steps and gazed across the sprawling, snow-covered lawn. "Your father and I were heartbroken when we realized that we had forgotten your birthday, and that you missed out on our family tradition. You poor thing, you must have felt wretched all day."

Charissa nodded, wiping her eyes with her sleeve, and described how horrible it felt that no one— not her parents, friends, or teachers—had acknowledged her birthday, and that she hadn't received a single slice of cake, dollop of ice cream, or birthday gift from anyone. Her careful preparations for a special and memorable fourteenth birthday had been wasted. Charissa's mother listened patiently and embraced her daughter securely as Charissa voiced her complaints about her horrible birthday.

"Come inside and I'll cook a special birthday dinner," her mother said as she turned the doorknob and stepped into the house, Charissa close behind. They entered the foyer, and as Charissa turned the corner and walked into the living room, she was greeted with a roomful of vibrant balloons and streamers, a huge banner that read "Happy 14th Birthday!" and a booming chorus of "SURPRISE!"

 Questions

1. What is Charissa's biggest problem in the story?

    A. She does not know what to wear on her birthday.
    B. Her mother does not give her a cupcake and a candle.
    C. Everyone she knows seems to have forgotten her birthday.
    D. She has trouble concentrating in science class.

 Tip

Think about the major conflict in the story. Which problem is emphasized?

2. Where does the beginning of the story take place?

    A. in Charissa's bedroom
    B. in Charissa's kitchen
    C. outside of a school
    D. on a school bus

 Tip

Reread the first paragraph of the story. Where is Charissa?

3. What happens at the end of the story that solves Charissa's problem?

    A. Her family throws her a party.
    B. Her mother apologizes to her.
    C. She tells her mother what happened.
    D. She smiles and hugs her mother.

 Tip

Think about Charissa's problem and what happens at the end of the story.

Check your answers on the next page.

Passage 2: "A Day to Remember"

 Answers

1. C   While all of these answer choices are problems Charissa faces during the day, only answer choice C tells her biggest problem. (Fiction)

2. A   Charissa is in her bedroom getting dressed in the beginning of the story. Therefore, answer choice A is correct. (Understanding a Text)

3. A   Charissa's problem is solved when she realizes that her family and friends have thrown her a surprise party and that they hadn't forgotten her birthday after all. (Understanding a Text)

Passage 3

Read the following passage and answer the questions that follow.

Mr. Salazar

Donning a new shirt and shorts and with his bookbag on his back, Seth proceeded toward the bus stop. *The first day of school is always a blast*, Seth thought. He was eagerly anticipating seeing some of his friends that he wasn't able to touch base with over summer vacation while he worked with his grandfather on his farm.

Seth felt certain that eighth grade was going to be his best year ever. As one of the oldest students, he knew nearly everyone in the school. He was going to be on the varsity basketball team and might even be chosen as a starter. The best part, however, would be having Mr. Jordan as his homeroom teacher.

Mr. Jordan had been Seth's English teacher for several years and Seth really enjoyed his classes, mainly because Mr. Jordan had an incredible sense of humor and managed to make learning great fun. After the class had read a new short story or novel, he would match students to characters and have the students act out a chapter or two. While at first Seth thought this would be extremely corny and contemplated outright refusing to comply with it, he changed his mind when Mr. Jordan assigned him the role of an old woman in one of Flannery O'Connor's short stories. Seth tried in vain to raise his deep voice so it resembled an old woman's, but all he managed to do was squeak—and make his classmates crack up with riotous laughter. Then Mr. Jordan assigned Seth's friend Charlie the part of a desk, which required Charlie to be quiet, a seemingly impossible task. Once everyone had their parts, they managed to get through it without laughing too loudly. Mr. Jordan discussed character motivation by asking each student (except Charlie) what made their character do the things that he or she did. In Seth's perception, Mr. Jordan was in the running for one of the world's greatest teachers.

This is why Seth was completely distraught to discover another man standing in front of Mr. Jordan's desk. "Who's *that*?" he asked his friend Ashley. "And why is he in Mr. Jordan's classroom leaning on his desk?" Ashley shook her head and told Seth she had no clue. The man was much younger than Mr. Jordan and, even though he hunched his shoulders and leaned forward slightly, he was much taller—too tall, in Seth's opinion. The man slipped his hands into his pockets nervously and smiled an awkward, crooked smile. When Seth's eyes met his, he nodded, but Seth was too bewildered to respond.

When everyone entered the room, the man introduced himself as Mr. Salazar. "Are you a substitute?" called out someone from the back of class.

Mr. Salazar shook his head negatively. "Mr. Jordan and his wife relocated to Philadelphia about a month ago, and I have been bestowed the honor of being your teacher this year."

While some students clapped and welcomed Mr. Salazar, Seth was too stunned to respond. His whole mood was stifled by the thought: *No more Mr. Jordan?* That meant no more funny plays, no joking around in class—learning would no longer be enjoyable. This man did not resemble Mr. Jordan in the slightest. He looked serious, nervous, and much too young to be a teacher. "Is this the first class you've ever taught?" Seth inquired.

Mr. Salazar laughed. "Yes," he replied. "I graduated college last May, but I student-taught during my last year and learned a great deal. I'm going to teach you many new and interesting things and we're going to have lots of fun learning."

Yeah, right, Seth thought. *This is going to ruin everything.*

Seth and his friend Charlie made a beeline for the basketball court at recess. Seth was surprised to see Mr. Salazar on the court dribbling a basketball. His lanky frame moved surprisingly swiftly as he approached the hoop. He reached up and gently shot the ball—*swish!* Mr. Salazar stopped when he saw them. "Hey boys, would you like to play?" he inquired.

Seth and Charlie approached him as two more boys walked onto the court. "You play basketball?" Seth asked him, surprised that someone who seemed so awkward and gangly would be involved in athletics.

"You bet!" replied Mr. Salazar enthusiastically. "I played in both high school and college."

Seth caught the rebound and tried unsuccessfully to pass by Mr. Salazar. Seth chuckled. "For a too-tall dude, you can really move," he joked. Mr. Salazar knocked the ball away from Seth and sunk it into the hoop. A crowd of students gathered around the court to watch Mr. Salazar's incredible skills. Seth's classmates attempted to defeat him in a lopsided four-on-one match, but it was to no avail. Exhausted, Seth plopped down on the side of the court. "You're so tall, no one can beat you," Seth said.

"Nah," Mr. Salazar replied and sunk yet another basket without breaking a sweat. "Size doesn't have all that much to do with it. Some of the best players on my college team were only average height, if not smaller. It's how you maneuver that makes the difference."

15 "You are really awesome," Seth said. "You are *really* awesome. Could you teach us to move like that?"

"Sure!" said Mr. Salazar. "I'm going to teach you lots of things—and not just about basketball. We're going to start a new novel in English today called *Dogsong*. Have you ever heard of it?"

Dogsong was written by Gary Paulsen, Seth's favorite author. Seth told Mr. Salazar about the other books he had read by Paulsen. When the bell rang ending recess, Seth headed back to class excited for the first time since he'd arrived at school. Maybe his fears weren't warranted and things weren't so bad after all.

? Questions

1. Seth's feelings change throughout the story. Compare how he feels when he first sees Mr. Salazar to how he feels at the end of the story. What happened to cause his feelings to change?

    Use details from the story to support your answer.

    _____

    _____

    _____

    _____

    _____

 Tip

Reread the story. Note Seth's feelings as the story progresses. What does Mr. Salazar do that causes Seth to admire him?

2. What did Seth like about Mr. Jordan?

    A. He made learning fun.
    B. He was extremely tall.
    C. He knew how to play basketball.
    D. He liked to read books by Gary Paulsen.

 Tip

Look back to the beginning of the story. What does Mr. Jordan do that makes Seth happy?

3.   What is Seth's main conflict in the story?

   A.   Mr. Salazar is too tall.
   B.   Mr. Jordan has moved away.
   C.   Seth wants to play basketball.
   D.   Seth is starting the eighth grade.

 Tip

Remember that the conflict is the biggest problem in the story. What is Seth's biggest problem?

4.   Why does the author repeat the same sentence in paragraph 15?

   A.   to emphasize that Seth is impressed with Mr. Salazar
   B.   to show that Seth likes being around Mr. Salazar
   C.   to show that Seth has listened carefully to Mr. Salazar
   D.   to emphasize that Seth is trying to get Mr. Salazar's attention

 Tip

Reread paragraph 15. Why would Seth say the same thing twice?

Check your answers on the next page. Read the explanation after each answer choice.

Passage 3: "Mr. Salazar"

 # Answers

1.   Your answer should compare how Seth feels when he first sees Mr. Salazar to how he feels at the end of the story and indicate what made his feelings change. (Fiction)

    Sample answer: Seth starts out very excited about the start of the school year because he will have his favorite teacher, Mr. Jordan, as homeroom teacher. He is surprised to discover another man in Mr. Jordan's classroom. When he learns that this man is taking Mr. Jordan's place, he does not think much of him. Mr. Salazar is young and awkward and Seth does not think he will be any good. Seth gets to know the new teacher better when he plays basketball with him, however, and his skill impresses Seth. Then Mr. Salazar tells Seth they are going to read a book by Gary Paulsen, Seth's favorite author. Seth's mood improves and he feels more willing to give Mr. Salazar a chance.

2.   A   In the beginning of the story, Seth says that Mr. Jordan was a great deal of fun and a good teacher. Answer choice A is correct. (Understanding a Text)

3.   B   The main conflict in this story is that Mr. Jordan has moved away, which means that Seth has a new teacher. Answer choice B is the best answer. (Fiction)

4.   A   By repeating the sentence and emphasizing the word "really," the author shows how impressed Seth is with Mr. Salazar. Answer choice A is correct. (Style and Language)

Passage 4

Read the passage and answer the questions that follow.

The Adventures of Gilgamesh

The people of Babylonia felt that their king, Gilgamesh, was a mixed blessing. On one hand, he was the mightiest and most influential king in the world. He was a hero of many battles, a son of the gods, and a man of endless intelligence and insight. He had envisioned and built the city of Uruk, a marvel of architecture with towering gates and brilliantly designed buildings. In the center of Uruk was a lapis lazuli, a gemstone with the proportions of a boulder. Carved into this stone were the chronicles of Gilgamesh's many adventures. Reading them over, nobody could deny that he had earned his fame.

However, Gilgamesh was also arrogant and brash, and frequently neglected the concerns of his people in order to concentrate on himself. On occasion he was downright oppressive, and when he began to interfere in citizens' marriages, the people decided something had to be done. They flocked to the temple and prayed to their chief god, Anu, pleading with him to confront Gilgamesh and end his exploitation. Their prayers were answered with silence, though, and the people left the temple disappointedly.

The next day, a hunter named Shuja headed into the forests outside the city in search of game. As soon as he stepped into the thick, shadowy woods, he heard an animal roar that he did not recognize. It resembled a horrifying combination of the growls, hoots, whistles, and barks of a dozen different species. He heard it again, and it was closer this time. Before he could evacuate, he found himself face-to-face with a hulking wild man surrounded by a team of vicious animals.

An hour later, an exhausted Shuja returned to the city. He looked so ragged and terrified that a crowd gathered around him, inquiring what troubles had befallen him. "I encountered a wild man in the forest, training animals for warfare," Shuja explained. "His name was Enkidu, and he said Anu had dispatched him to dethrone King Gilgamesh."

5   A worried murmur passed through the crowd. What would happen if such a menacing creature attacked Uruk, they wondered. The prospect was even less pleasant than the prospect of Gilgamesh's continued oppression. They realized they needed to stop Enkidu, but how could they negotiate with an animal-like man? Some thought they should fight; some thought they should flee. Some thought they should surrender to the creature and some believed they could reason with it. Nobody could agree on a course of action.

"Stop this quarreling; I'll solve this predicament," announced Shamhat, one of the most beautiful women in Uruk. The next morning she left the city's protective walls and proceeded into the forest in search of Enkidu. She found him at a watering hole where he and his supporters had bivouacked. Shamhat approached him, and he could sense that she was not motivated by apprehension or hostility. This caught Enkidu off guard.

Shamhat addressed Enkidu with kindness and compassion, and he responded in a similarly civil manner. They spent the day together and, the next morning, she led him into Uruk as a friend, not an enemy. The people gathered around them and celebrated the cessation of his threat. Enkidu, though disoriented by the new environment, came to love the beauty, companionship, and sophistication he encountered inside the city walls. Taking up residence with some shepherds, Enkidu learned how to behave like a civilized human being.

Meanwhile, Gilgamesh had been having visions of powerful, mysterious newcomers trespassing upon his land. It was therefore no surprise to him to learn of Enkidu's presence in Uruk. Gilgamesh consulted with his mother, who advised him to embrace this newcomer as a friend, because together they were destined for great accomplishments.

"What does she know?" Gilgamesh thought bitterly. *"I would not degrade myself by accepting some wild man as a companion."*

And so Gilgamesh continued his oppression of the people. During a marriage celebration, Gilgamesh interfered again. He was jealous of the groom and intended to kidnap the bride. He believed he was justified in doing so because he was the ruler of Uruk, and he was comfortable with the knowledge that nobody would challenge him. But he'd forgotten about the newcomer, Enkidu, who suddenly appeared in the king's doorway and refused to allow him to break up the wedding.

"How dare you exploit your people for your own gain?" demanded Enkidu.

"How dare you question my decisions?" roared Gilgamesh, lunging forward to attack his challenger.

The two combatants struggled for hours, their powers equally balanced. Finally, Gilgamesh was able to secure an advantage in the battle, and raised a sword high over Enkidu. Instead of bringing the sword slashing down, though, he paused and then slowly lowered the weapon.

"You are a worthy opponent," he admitted, "and I was wrong to belittle you. I see the wisdom in your challenge, and I will not spoil the wedding." Gilgamesh helped Enkidu to his feet, and then they shook hands. "I think my mother was right. If you and I work together, we can accomplish great things for the people of Uruk."

Gilgamesh and Enkidu became fast friends, and they enjoyed one another's company for many weeks. Soon, however, the pair began to feel restless in the tranquil city of Uruk. They yearned for adventures in the mysterious lands outside the city walls. "Every day we reside within these walls, we grow increasingly accustomed to peace and quiet," complained Gilgamesh. "We're losing our power and energy! Another month of this and there will be nothing to separate us from regular farmers and townspeople."

Enkidu agreed enthusiastically. He'd learned the lifestyles of civilized humans, but in his soul he felt a longing to be wild and free again. "Yes!" he roared, sounding for a moment almost like a bear. "Let's strike off into the forests and find new, undiscovered horizons!"

Gilgamesh began to envision this grand new adventure. He had a faraway look on his face as though, in his imagination, he was already tromping toward a new glorious goal. For a while, he even seemed unaware that Enkidu was watching him curiously. When Enkidu finally asked, "What are you thinking about?" Gilgamesh woke abruptly from his daydream.

"Enkidu, my friend, I have conceived of the greatest adventure ever undertaken. I propose that you and I leave tomorrow for the great Cedar Forest."

Immediately, Enkidu's enthusiasm waned. His face looked timid for the first time ever when he whimpered, "But, Gilgamesh—that's the land of the demon Humbaba the Terrible. He surely would destroy any trespassers there."

Gilgamesh laughed brazenly. "Not if we destroy him first! I propose that we do battle with Humbaba, send him back to the underworld, and claim his forest for the people of Uruk!"

Enkidu was not to be convinced. "I must protest, Gilgamesh. Do not mistake me for a coward when I say this, but during my years in the forests I've heard many horrifying tales of Humbaba. I am convinced that as an enemy he is beyond parallel. I have great faith in you, and in myself, but I doubt that even together we could defeat the likes of Humbaba."

"Nonsense," laughed Gilgamesh. "Do not hamper my spirit with your doubt. Together we will find and defeat this menace, and put the legends of his invincibility to rest forever!"

Despite Enkidu's continued warnings, Gilgamesh assembled the people of Uruk in the city center the next day to announce his plans. He climbed to the top of the lapis lazuli, and from there he addressed his audience. King Gilgamesh reminded them that his many great deeds were engraved all over the stone, but told them that his upcoming deed would outshine all of them. The people cheered for him, and then begged for an explanation.

In a voice strong and thick with confidence, Gilgamesh told them his plan. Before his eyes, the people went pale with fear. Some shuddered, or whispered worriedly to one another.

"What is that murmuring?" he demanded angrily. "Why the looks of apprehension? Do you people not have faith in your king?"

"We do, sire," called out a shepherd, "That's why we don't want to lose you to that fiend Humbaba."

Gilgamesh was appalled that his own subjects considered him less powerful than Humbaba. Angrily he stormed off the lapis lazuli and headed toward the armory, where he gathered the finest swords and armor in the kingdom. When he returned, he found Enkidu, gave him half of the equipment, and said simply, "Be prepared to leave at dawn." Then Gilgamesh retired to his palace.

The people swarmed around Enkidu, begging him to bring King Gilgamesh back to his senses. Enkidu insisted that there was no hope of that; the king was determined to confront the demon Humbaba. The people reluctantly accepted this truth, but they implored Enkidu to do all he could to protect their beloved king. Even Gilgamesh's mother arrived at the town center to plead with Enkidu. The warrior agreed that he would do everything he could do.

"Though I do not agree with his decision, Gilgamesh remains my most loyal friend. During our battle with Humbaba, I will stand in the forward position to guard the king's life. If Humbaba makes a killer blow, it will be my life that is lost, and Gilgamesh will have time to escape back to Uruk."

The people cheered Enkidu's heroic pledge, but it was with lingering worry that they watched the duo march out of the city walls the next morning. Gilgamesh and Enkidu walked into the forests and proceeded for six days without facing any physical obstacles. The only threats came in their dreams; Gilgamesh was tortured each night by dreams of death and disaster. He dreamt of a giant bull which tramples him and Uruk, and then he dreamt of a storm that rips the world apart. The king's dreams became so vivid and awful that his confidence began to wane.

Enkidu saw the danger in this. The warriors were already deep in the Cedar Forest, where Humbaba could strike at any moment. If Gilgamesh were to become weak with fright, they would both surely be destroyed. So, when Enkidu heard the king's dreams, he tried to interpret them positively. He convinced Gilgamesh that his dreams were signs from the gods that he would be protected during the upcoming battle. Gilgamesh was not completely convinced of this, but Enkidu's faith in him and his spirit of friendship restored Gilgamesh's confidence.

As they approached Humbaba's lair—close enough to smell his foul stench nearby—Enkidu began to tremble with fear. Now he was the one to lose his nerve, and he turned and attempted to retreat. Gilgamesh ran after him, not to join in the retreat, but to catch him and urge him forward again. "We cannot turn back now!" Gilgamesh called after him. After a short chase, he pulled Enkidu to the ground. "We're too close to go back now, Enkidu. To turn our backs on this creature would be asking for attack—"

And indeed it was, for during their scuffle, Humbaba had appeared behind them. The demon was a hideous beast. He was broad and heavy as a rhinoceros, with a head the size of a boulder. His arms and legs were each as big as a bull and his face was a horrid mask of evil. Humbaba let out a mighty growl: "Who are you to trespass in my forest?" Then he pulled a tree up from its roots and swung it at them. "I'll destroy you both, like I have every past intruder."

"Remember your courage, Enkidu," Gilgamesh pleaded. "We must face this threat as one—it's the only way!" In a second, he saw the bravery flickering back into Enkidu's eyes. Enkidu nodded his agreement, and then the two warriors stood up together. They faced the demon and brandished their swords.

They did so just in time to block a furious attack by Humbaba, who swung the tree again with a mighty grunt. While Humbaba was preparing to swing again, Gilgamesh and Enkidu sprang on him with their swords. Humbaba growled and wildly lashed out with his pig-sized fists; he struck Gilgamesh, who tumbled back into the bushes. As Humbaba turned to attack the injured king, Enkidu moved quickly in his defense. While Enkidu struggled with the demon, Gilgamesh regained his strength and returned to the combat.

Soon, Humbaba was overwhelmed by the two warriors, and Enkidu was able to strike him down. As Humbaba collapsed, he gasped, "A thousand curses on you, Enkidu! May you find no peace in this world!" Then the horrible demon crumbled away, and his menace was gone forever from the Cedar Forest.

As soon as they'd caught their breath, Gilgamesh and Enkidu let out a cheer of triumph. They shook hands and congratulated one another on their great victory, and the strengthening of their friendship. Together, they proceeded to cut some trees and make a boat for the long journey back to Uruk.

Questions

1. Why were the people of Babylon upset with King Gilgamesh?

    A. He forbade them to pray to Anu.
    B. He listened to his mother's advice.
    C. He made friends with a wild man.
    D. He interfered in wedding ceremonies.

Tip

If you don't recall this detail, look back to the beginning of the story.

2. Why didn't Gilgamesh want to make friends with Enkidu?

    A. He was afraid of Enkidu.
    B. His mother warned against it.
    C. He knew Enkidu wanted to be king.
    D. He thought he was better than Enkidu.

Tip

Think about when Gilgamesh first learned about Enkidu. What was his attitude toward the wild man?

3. Gilgamesh relied on Enkidu's help to defeat Humbaba.

    *   How did Enkidu restore Gilgamesh's confidence?
    *   How did Enkidu and Gilgamesh use teamwork to accomplish their goal?

    Use details and information from the story to support your answer.

    _____

    _____

    _____

Tip

Reread the part of the story where Gilgamesh and Enkidu set out to battle Humbaba. How did their cooperation bring them victory?

4.   How did Enkidu change after meeting Shamhat?

    A.   from noble to selfish

    B.   from brave to cowardly

    C.   from untamed to mannerly

    D.   from peace-loving to warlike

Tip

Think about how Enkidu acted before meeting the beautiful Shamhat, and then how he transformed afterwards.

5.   In paragraph 5, in the sentence that ends " . . . but how could they negotiate with an animal-like man?"—"animal-like" is used as

    A.   an adjective.

    B.   a noun.

    C.   a prepositional phrase.

    D.   an adverb.

Tip

Does "animal-like" describe a word in the sentence? If so, what part of speech is that word?

Check your answers on the next page. Read the explanation after each answer choice.

Passage 4: "The Adventures of Gilgamesh"

 **Answers**

1. D Early in the story, the people of Uruk were very upset with King Gilgamesh because he often interfered in the people's wedding ceremonies. (Myth)

2. D Although Gilgamesh's mother advised that he make friends with Enkidu, Gilgamesh at first refused to do so. He felt that he was too good to be friends with a wild man like Enkidu. (Myth)

3. **Sample answer:** Enkidu followed King Gilgamesh on the journey into the Cedar Forest and was crucial to their victory over Humbaba. When the king had horrifying nightmares about deadly bulls and storms, Enkidu consoled him and said the dreams meant that the gods would protect him. Enkidu's loyal friendship gave Gilgamesh courage. Later, both Gilgamesh and Enkidu lost their nerve and wanted to retreat, but they decided to cooperate. They worked together to destroy the demon. (Understanding a Text)

4. C Before meeting Shamhat, Enkidu ran untamed in the forests with the animals. By showing him kindness, Shamhat helped him transform into a mannerly citizen. (Understanding a Text)

5. A "Animal-like" is used as an adjective to modify the noun, "man." (Style and Language)

Lesson 6: Drama

This lesson covers the following standards for Grade 7: English Language Arts, Language, and Literature:

- Reading and Literature Strand
  - Standard 8: Understanding a Text
  - Standard 17: Dramatic Literature

What Is the Role of Imagination In Drama?

For the most part, dramatic literature is meant to be performed rather than just read. The effectiveness of the message of the play, movie, or TV show—as well as its entertainment value—depends on the actors who interpret the lines of dialogue with their expressions and gestures. Reading dramatic fiction, therefore, requires an active imagination.

For the passage that follows, try to picture the characters as they might look in front of you on a stage or screen. Assign roles to professional actors or to people you know. Imagine the surroundings (settings) for the action. The author gives us just the basic information in the stage directions set off in brackets { }. You have to provide the rest.

After the brief scenes that follow, you'll be asked a few questions over what happens between the characters. You'll also be asked to speculate about what could happen based on your reading and your own experience.

Passage 1

Read the following passage and answer the questions that follow.

Aunt Flo's Cafe

Adapted from *You're Never Really Alone*
By Glenn Morrison

{Scene: In the kitchen of a small cafe during the lunch rush. A young woman enters and is greeted by a young man in kitchen whites.}

Teddy: Cassie! Cassie! Hello Cassie!

Cassie: Hello Teddy. Feeling good today?

Teddy: I always feel good, Cassie, especially when we are so nice and busy.

{Florence Untermyer enters. She is a big woman with a lot of energy}

Flo: Cassie! Grab an apron and help Gert out front, will ya? Teddy, go bus some tables and get the dishwasher going. Hurry now.

Teddy: Yes, yes, great lady. I go.

Cassie: Where's Luther, Aunt Flo? And Merelee?

Flo: Luther got drunk again last night and fell off their front porch. Broke his hip and I don't know what else. Merelee is with him at the hospital, giving him Hell probably. Listen, little girl, if ever you run a business, never hire both the husband and the wife. If one of them is out, then the other is, too.

Cassie: Why, Aunt Flo, you know you told me hiring Merelee was the best thing you ever did because she got Luther here every day.

Flo: Go on. You can bother me about this later. Now I got to do all the cooking.

Cassie: I can help, Aunt Flo.

Flo: Oh please, let's not make anyone else ill. Just take a few tables and send Gert in for a couple minutes. And don't let Teddy talk to the customers.

{Scene: It is mid-afternoon, and the place is calm. Flo is on the phone to Earl's Appliance Repair.)

Flo: No. Teddy did not break the dishwasher. It just doesn't work right. Maybe. But he's not as dumb as some people I could name . . . Well, I don't feel very sweet today, Earl. No stories, Earl. No excuses, ok? . . . Earl, you're commencing to annoy me . . . If Untermyer were still alive, you wouldn't ask that . . . Uh uh. Just get out here to fix the machine before supper.

Cassie: Can I help, Aunt Flo?

Flo: Yes. Be nice to that fool Earl when he comes to fix the dishwasher. But don't let him get any ideas.

{Much later and the dinner customers are gone. Flo, Cassie, and Gert—a very tired looking woman in her 40s—are sitting around a table. Gert is shuffling a deck of playing cards.}

<u>Flo</u>: Ladies, a day like today makes me wish we had a good man around here.

<u>Cassie</u>: That's hardly special. You wish that most days.

<u>Gert</u>: There are no good men.

<u>Flo</u>: Untermyer was a good man. He'd stand up for you. He'd be around when there was work, not just for food and fun. He could handle jerks like Earl. You wouldn't even have to think about them.

<u>Gert</u>: Maybe you got lucky once, Florence. It's been my sad experience that men are like Luther or Teddy. Worthless drunks or big foolish boys. Or both. Who needs 'em?

<u>Cassie</u>: Luther and Teddy are all right.

<u>Flo</u>: You think everybody is all right, youngster. But a good man like Untermyer takes care of things.

<u>Gert</u>: Seems to me you take care of things pretty well on your own, Florence.

<u>Flo</u>: Life should be easier, Gert old gal. A woman should have a man who appreciates her and who can deal with some of the messy business of living. Like my Untermyer.

<u>Gert</u>: Men make messes! Women clean them up!

<u>Flo</u>: Not saying you're wrong, Gert old gal. I'm only saying there ought to be more to a man than messes and aggravation.

{Flo slaps the table, ending the conversation. Gert deals the cards.}

 **Questions**

1. Florence Untermyer (Aunt Flo)

   A. is Teddy's mother.
   B. was once married to a man named Untermyer.
   C. is going out with Earl.
   D. does not want anything to do with men.

 Tip
Review the conversation at the card table.

2. Which man is correctly matched with the reason why the women are upset?

    A.   Luther because he was injured while drunk and missed work.

    B.   Teddy because he was taking drugs.

    C.   Earl because he never fixed the dishwashing machine.

    D.   An unnamed customer who didn't pay his bill.

 Tip

Why do the women have to do more work than usual?

3. Briefly compare and contrast the attitude of Cassie, Flo, and Gert toward men. Cite one line for each from the scenes shown.

_____

_____

_____

_____

4. Who do you think would be most likely to forgive Luther when he comes back? Who would be least likely to forgive him? Cite lines from the play to support your answer.

_____

_____

_____

_____

Passage 1: "Aunt Flo's Café"

 **Answers**

1. B   Flo was married to a man named Untermyer, and she'd like to have another "good man" like him in her life. She doesn't get along with Earl. There is no evidence that Teddy is her son. (Understanding a Text)

2. A   They are all upset that Luther was injured and missed work. There is no evidence that Teddy was on drugs or that any customer walked out without paying. Earl evidently fixed the machine because they certainly would have said something if he had not. (Dramatic Literature)

3. **Sample Answer:** Gert had no use for men at all ("Men make messes. Women clean them up"). Cassie was OK with everybody ("You think everyone's alright, youngster). Flo makes the distinction between "good men" and the mess-making kind ("He'd be around when there was work, not just for fun and food"). (Dramatic Literature)

4. **Sample Answer:** Gert doesn't seem the forgiving kind, although she doesn't expect much of men in the first place. Cassie would certainly forgive Luther, but she would probably want to have a talk with him. Flo might forgive him out of necessity, and she certainly would have things to say to him—and his wife. (Dramatic Literature)

POSTTEST

POSTTEST

Part A: Composition

WRITING: SESSION 1

DIRECTIONS

In this first session of Part A, you will be asked to write an initial draft of a persuasive essay. Plan and draft your answer on a separate piece of paper. If you finish ahead of time, do not go on to the next part of the test. Wait for your teacher to continue.

Writing Prompt

WRITING PROMPT

Your parents arrived home from last night's city council meeting upset that the council is planning to cut down a century-old oak tree in the middle of the town square to make room for a new movie theater. The council members feel the tree's large branches are a danger to electrical lines and telephone poles, and they think the space could be utilized to build a movie theater that would bring more revenue into the city. Many city residents, however, think that the tree is a part of your town's heritage, and that cutting it down will only destroy what little history your town has left.

The council has decided to make its official decision on the removal of the tree after they hold a vote and get more feedback from the residents of the city. You decide to write the editor of your local newspaper about this decision.

Write a letter to the local newspaper explaining your position on this issue. Use facts and examples to develop your argument.

PREWRITING/PLANNING SPACE

DIRECTIONS

When you finish your planning, write your first draft on the lined page that follows.

Part A: Composition

REVISING: SESSION 2

DIRECTIONS

To complete this part of the test, you will revise and edit the draft you wrote in the first session. Copy your final draft on the lined page that follows.

Part B

LANGUAGE AND LITERATURE: SESSION 1

DIRECTIONS

This session contains reading selections with multiple-choice questions and open-response questions. Mark your answers to these questions on the Answer Sheets provided.

Learning to accept criticism can be difficult. Here is a story about a boy who asks his grandfather to critique his writing.

Ouch!

1   Enrico slipped off his jacket and tossed it on the lawn beside him. The bright sun had warmed the chilly morning air. Enrico picked up a marigold and began removing the dirt around its roots before placing it into one of the shallow holes he and his grandfather had dug. "No, no, Enrico, don't do that," his grandfather gently chided. "It's better to leave the root ball intact. If you break off the soil, you might damage the roots and kill the plant."

2   Enrico smiled and placed the flower in the hole with the roots and surrounding soil intact. His grandfather, his abuelo, was a man of great experience and wisdom. He had taught Enrico many things throughout the years. He had taught him the importance of using good-quality lumber when they built a garden shed together in the backyard. Under his grandfather's guidance, Enrico had learned how to make the world's greatest tortillas using peppers so hot they burned your lips. Most of the novels Enrico devoured at night were his grandfather's picks. Grandfather often recommended a new read for Enrico, usually one that was obscure but wonderful, the kind of book you might find at a yard sale rather than on a bestsellers list.

3   Now Enrico wanted his grandfather to teach him how to be a better writer. Even though he had learned English as a second language, Grandfather had become adept enough to publish several history books and had worked for many years as a news reporter for their local paper. "I want to be a writer," Enrico announced as he gently pushed the soil around the marigold so it stood straight in its new home. "I've actually written several short stories. I was hoping you would read them and tell me what you think— and not just tell me that they're good. I want your guidance, so I can improve my writing abilities and become a published writer."

4   Grandfather shook his head. "Ah, I don't know, Enrico. It isn't easy having your writing critiqued, and I wouldn't want to chance hurting your feelings. You're a bright young man. If you choose to become a writer, you will be a good one, with or without my help."

5   Despite his grandfather's warnings, however, Enrico finally persuaded him to critique one of his short stories. Enrico selected his best piece: a tale about a boy who was the smallest and worst player on his basketball team. The boy, Miguel, was often teased by the other players for his lack of height and skill. Enrico had revised the story several times until he was certain that his command of the English language was at its best. He printed a copy of the story and left it on his grandfather's kitchen table with a note on top that said, "Tell the truth, Grandfather. I can take it, really I can. And I greatly appreciate your help."

6   After school the next day Enrico rushed to his grandfather's house. "Did you read it?" he

asked, as his grandfather rubbed a wet dish with a towel and placed it on a shelf.

7   "Of course I read it, son," Grandfather said and grinned, "and I think you're a very good writer."

8   Feeling frustrated, Enrico sighed and plopped in a kitchen chair. This was not what he wanted to hear. "Could you give me more than that?" he asked as he ran his fingers through his hair. "Could you tell me what is good about the story and what is bad? Please?"

9   Grandfather pulled out a chair and sat down beside Enrico. He picked up the printout of Enrico's story. "You need to show more and tell less, for starters," Grandfather advised. "For example, don't tell the reader that Miguel had a sad look on his face. What about Miguel's face looked sad? Describe his face and let your readers draw their own conclusion." Enrico nodded. "And your plot is so predictable that I knew Miguel was going to score the winning basket after reading only the first paragraph.

Why not have him miss the shot, but impress his teammates with his newly acquired skill?"

10   Enrico frowned. "Ouch!" he exclaimed. "Wasn't there *anything* you liked about my story?"

11   Grandfather laughed loudly. "I told you it's tough to hear criticism regarding your writing. Writing is a process and, as a writer, your work must undergo many revisions. This is normal, Enrico."

12   "Maybe I don't have the talent to become a published writer," Enrico confessed, doubting himself.

13   "You definitely have the talent, but do you have the perseverance? Great writers do not give up. They keep on revising until they get it right."

14   Enrico smiled. "I hear what you're saying and I won't give up. I'm ready to try again, and I will keep trying until my work is as good as it can be," Enrico said. Grandfather shook his hand. "That's my boy," he said. "I am very proud of you."

1 Why doesn't Grandfather want to read Enrico's story?

    A. He does not think it will be any good.

    B. He does not enjoy suggesting changes.

    C. He does not want to hurt Enrico's feelings.

    D. He does not believe Enrico will listen to him.

2 Read this sentence from the story.

"No, no, Enrico, don't do that," his grandfather gently chided.

What does the word *chided* mean?

    A. claimed

    B. corrected

    C. concealed

    D. challenged

3 What is one problem with the story Enrico has written?

    A. The outcome is obvious.

    B. The first paragraph is too long.

    C. The main character is ordinary.

    D. The language needs improvement.

4 The title of the story, "Ouch!" captures

    A. how Grandfather feels.

    B. how Enrico feels.

    C. the title of Enrico's story.

    D. how Miguel feels.

5 How does Enrico feel about his Grandfather?

    A. sympathetic

    B. annoyed

    C. suspicious

    D. appreciative

6 Which technique does the author use to establish the theme of this passage?

    A. repetition

    B. personification

    C. dialogue

    D. flashback

Write your answer to open-response question 7 in the space provided in the Answer Sheets.

 In the beginning of the story the author says that Grandfather learned English as a second language and that he "had become adept enough to publish several history books and had worked for many years as a news reporter for their local paper."

- Tell why the author included this detail.
- Explain how this detail relates to the central idea of the story.

Use information and details from the story to support your answer.

Read the following persuasive passage and then answer the questions that follow it.

Edentown Editorials
Save Culture in our Cities—Support Funding for the Arts!

1 Recently, in many areas of our country, those who look around may notice the absence of the cultural outlets that once were very special parts of cities, both small and large. Theater companies have packed up their productions and vacated their tiny theater spaces, small galleries have rejected mass quantities of artwork that they cannot house, and annual dance performances have been cancelled. This depletion of culture is due to one simple fact: funding for the arts is being cut in vast amounts, leaving many artists without the means to survive.

2 Arts and humanities are critically important to communities, especially those smaller communities lacking an abundance of cultural resources and improvements. It goes without saying that communities and their members are enhanced—on both group and personal levels—by exposure to artistic mediums. In recent years, community attention as a whole has been deflected away from the arts and has instead focused on popular culture such as trendy cinema, reality television programs, magazines devoted to revealing personal information about celebrities, and so on. While each of these media offers something of value to communities—no matter how slight it may seem—it is only when balanced with different and truly educational forms of entertainment that we can see this value. When one side of the cultural equation—here, the arts—diminishes, communities are forced to depend on the other side—popular culture entertainment—to fulfill their identities as cultural communities. This can never occur, however, because the arts are much more valuable than the popular distractions communities are left with when their artists are forced to take residence in areas where they can earn enough money to survive.

3 Even more problematic is the fact that artists are finding fewer areas of the country willing to integrate their art forms into communities, or to even view their art as valuable enough to warrant being included in the communities. During the last few years, more states have cut budgets that have supported artists in the past. For example, when an eighteen-million-dollar budget that formerly supported seven hundred artists' groups is cut down to less than a quarter of the former budget (say, two million dollars), these groups can no longer continue to provide their communities with culturally boosting artistic creations. This is happening all over the country and is worsening every year. And when state governors start considering the possibility of eliminating State Arts Councils (which collect funds and distribute them to appropriate groups), artists' groups are left floundering on their own.

4 Not every state has disowned its artists, and this minority should be commended. Pennsylvania's state government, for example,

has maintained its funding for the arts at consistent levels for years, and though New York state has had to lower the amount of money it contributes to its artists, the cut was much less drastic than cuts in the majority of other states. When state governments take away the majority of the money that supports their artists, they are essentially stating that these particular government officials do not consider the arts to be a valuable element of their communities.

5   Though state government officials play a huge role in this predicament, the problem does not rest entirely in their hands. Funding for the arts comes from several different levels, with the largest distributor being the federal government and the smallest being private, individual donations. However, when state governments fail, they place the financial shortage in the laps of local and public arts agencies, who struggle to raise money from corporations and private citizens regardless of the amount of state support.

6   We, as a national community, need to redefine what we value, as well as invent more creative ways to raise money to support the existence of art in communities. For example, the state of California raised money for the arts by selling license plates designed by a respected pop artist, and the state of Massachusetts directed a percentage of its lottery profits to its artistic community. Other states have taxed out-of-state corporations and businesses conducting business in their state and have given this money to state arts agencies, which distribute it to their artists. Some states have imposed a tax on those living in specific districts of major metropolitan areas, districts primarily dedicated to and influenced by the arts, in order to keep the theme and tone of such districts. Hotel and motel taxes, entertainment taxes, and other varied taxes have also been implemented for the purpose of supporting the arts. States implementing these taxes have been successful in raising money for the arts, but the fact remains that funding in most of these states is less than half of what it used to be, and that more effort on the part of governments and their citizens is necessary.

7   Perhaps if the majority of state governments were more supportive of their artists—as the previously mentioned progressive states have been—more of their citizens would make personal efforts to hold onto community gems such as local theaters, progressive art exhibitions, and unique literary publications. A large amount of arts funding comes from corporate, foundation, and individual donations. Are we to expect these groups to value and support the arts when so many of our state governments, in essence, view the arts as worthless?

8   The arts are by no means worthless. Artistic forms expose people both young and old to new experiences, broadening their cultural horizons while educating in a way that no other medium can. They become identifying factors for communities and help to develop individuals' identities and educations as well. The arts reach out to people of all ages—from developing children learning to appreciate the carefully crafted plot of a good book or the majestic colors and speckled images in an impressionist painting, to twenty-something young adults discovering their passions and talents by experimenting with the art forms around them, to middle-aged adults seeking distraction from their busy lives by attending a play or poetry reading, to senior citizens sparked by the comfort of a familiar song, piece of prose, or painting. If more citizens are made aware of the dismal situation of funding for the arts in their own communities, and if more people learn to view the arts as a valuable community asset, perhaps this situation can be reversed.

8 Which of the following contributes MOST to the lack of arts in many cities?

   A. a decrease in private funding

   B. a decrease in government funding

   C. a lack of space devoted to arts

   D. a change in people's values concerning art

9 What does <u>vacated</u> mean in the first paragraph?

   A. sold

   B. left

   C. closed

   D. relocated

10 Which experience would BEST help you gain an appreciation for the artistic culture the author refers to?

   A. watching a popular movie

   B. reading a celebrity magazine

   C. viewing reality television

   D. attending a poetry reading

11 Why did the author write this article?

   A. to inform readers about the plight of many artists

   B. to describe the effects of popular culture on society

   C. to persuade readers that funding for the arts is important

   D. to explain why artists must leave smaller communities

12 Which detail supports the author's main idea?

   A. Some states have disowned their artists.

   B. Popular and artistic culture can exist in the same city.

   C. Communities suffer when they lose artists.

   D. People should attend shows at art galleries.

13 In the last paragraph the hyphenated words "twenty-something" and "middle-aged" are used as

   A. adjectives.

   B. adverbs.

   C. nouns.

   D. prepositional phrases.

Write your answer to open-response question 14 in the space provided on the Answer Sheets.

14   Imagine that you disagree with the author's position on the arts.

- Describe a counterargument that you might present to disagree with the author.

- What kind of person would be likely to disagree with the author's opinion on funding the arts?

Use information and details from the article to support your answer.

In this part of the test, you will read a passage containing informational/everyday text and then respond to the multiple-choice questions that follow. You may look back at the passage and make notes in your test booklet if you like.

Fin-tastic Savings!

When it comes to your underwater pets, you don't have to settle for anything less than the best. Starting January 15, Main Avenue Pet Supplies will be offering top name-brand aquarium equipment—everything you need to set up a great aquarium at discount prices. Here are just a few of the items in our inventory:

Starter Aquariums
2.5 gallon - $19.99
5 gallon - $29.99

Water Filter
Was $26.99,
now only $19.99!

Goldfish - $1.25 each

Floating Thermometer - $5.99

Aquarium Accessories – $4.99 to $10.99

Main Avenue Pet Supplies
7701 Main Avenue, Springfield
Open M-F 10-5, Saturday 12-4.

The Ins and Outs of Aquariums

1   Have you ever had a flippered friend? Over the last century, fish have consistently been one of America's most preferred pets. Compared to most popular domestic animals, fish are low-maintenance creatures. They're well-behaved, too. They won't gnaw on furniture, shred curtains, or shed fur!

2   Setting up an aquarium can be an enjoyable project that calls on you not only to choose the conditions that would most benefit the fish, but also to make creative decisions that turn an aquarium into a piece of aquatic art. In order to construct an aquarium that's safe for fish and pleasing to the eye, follow these general guidelines. For more specific information, consult a specialist at your local pet shop.

3   You'll need a number of materials in order to get started. The most important item is, of course, the aquarium itself. Aquariums come in all shapes and sizes, from small one-gallon fishbowls meant for a single swimmer to giant tanks that can hold dozens of them.

4   After you've chosen the best aquarium, you'll need some special equipment to make it a safe and healthy habitat for your fish. You'll need aquarium gravel, a water filter, a water heater, a floating thermometer, and a pump.

5   Once you've acquired the necessary materials, the first step is to cleanse the aquarium of any grime, sediments, or other refuse that may have accumulated in it. Avoid using cleaning chemicals, though, since they can contaminate the water you later add to the aquarium. Once the aquarium is clean, add gravel to the bottom, typically one pound per gallon of water. You can even accessorize your aquarium with rocks, plants, or fanciful ornaments.

6   You'll want to install a filter in order to remove contaminants from the water and keep your fish healthy. Select a filter that's suitable for the size of your aquarium, and then install it according to the directions.

7   The next step is to fill the aquarium with clean, cool water; a safe guideline here is to only utilize water that you would consider drinkable. Don't fill the aquarium right to the top, though, because there are still a few subsequent items you'll need to add, including the water heater and pump. Install these appliances according to their directions. Usually, the heater should be adjusted to keep the water at a temperature of about seventy-five degrees Fahrenheit.

8   Then the fish will be more comfortable and healthy—unless you forget to add them! The most crucial component of an aquarium is, of course, the fish. Add them to the water and enjoy your new flippered friends.

15 What does the word <u>habitat</u> mean in paragraph 4?

   A. environment

   B. location

   C. temperature

   D. lifespan

16 The advertisement was probably designed by a

   A. store clerk.

   B. fish expert.

   C. salesperson.

   D. pet lover.

17 The paragraph at the top of the ad suggests that Main Avenue Pet Supplies

   A. has a wide variety of merchandise.

   B. sells high-quality merchandise.

   C. is well-known for its fish supplies.

   D. sells many different kinds of fish.

18 The author begins the passage with a question to

   A. show that fish are friendly.

   B. get the reader's attention.

   C. introduce an explanation.

   D. provide background information.

19 Which word best describes the author's tone in the first paragraph?

   A. serious

   B. humorous

   C. sentimental

   D. objective

20 According to the advertisement, the most expensive item you will need to start an aquarium is the

   A. tank.

   B. filter.

   C. fish.

   D. thermometer.

LANGUAGE AND LITERATURE: SESSION 2

DIRECTIONS
This session contains reading selections with multiple-choice questions and one open-response question. Mark your answers to these questions on the Answer Sheets provided.

This excerpt is from the book Incidents in the Life of a Slave Girl, *in which Harriet Jacobs tells the story of how she struggled for freedom from slavery and a reunion with her children. It is one of the few narratives of slavery written by a woman. In this excerpt, Jacobs has gone into hiding after living with a cruel master.*

Excerpt from *Incidents in the Life of a Slave Girl*
by Harriet Jacobs

1   **MUCH AS I DESPISE AND DETEST** the class of slave-traders, whom I regard as the vilest wretches on earth, I must do this man the justice to say that he seemed to have some feeling. He took a fancy to William in the jail, and wanted to buy him. When he heard the story of my children, he was willing to aid them in getting out of Dr. Flint's power, even without charging the customary fee.

2   My uncle procured a wagon and carried William and the children back to town. Great was the joy in my grandmother's house! The curtains were closed, and the candles lighted. The happy grandmother cuddled the little ones to her bosom. They hugged her, and kissed her, and clapped their hands, and shouted. She knelt down and poured forth one of her heartfelt prayers of thanksgiving to God. The father was present for a while; and though such a "parental relation" as existed between him and my children takes slight hold of the hearts or consciences of slaveholders, it must be that he experienced some moments of pure joy in witnessing the happiness he had imparted.

3   I had no share in the rejoicings of that evening.

4   The events of the day had not come to my knowledge. And now I will tell you something that happened to me; though you will, perhaps, think it illustrates the superstition of slaves. I sat in my usual place on the floor near the window, where I could hear much that was said in the street without being seen. The family had retired for the night, and all was still. I sat there thinking of my children, when I heard a low strain of music. A band of serenaders were under the window, playing "Home, sweet home." I listened till the sounds did not seem like music, but like the moaning of children. It seemed as if my heart would burst. I rose from my sitting posture, and knelt. A streak of moonlight was on the floor before me, and in the midst of it appeared the forms of my two children. They vanished; but I had seen them distinctly. Some will call it a dream, others a vision. I know not how to account for it, but it made a strong impression on my mind, and I felt certain something had happened to my little ones. . . .

5   At dawn, Betty was up and off to the kitchen. The hours passed on, and the vision of the night kept constantly recurring to my thoughts. After a while I heard the voices of two women in the entry. In one of them I recognized the housemaid. The other said to her, "Did you know Linda Brent's children was sold to the speculator[1] yesterday? They say ole massa Flint was mighty glad to see 'em drove out of town; but they say they've come back again. I 'spect it's all their daddy's doings. They say he's bought William too. Lor! how it will take hold of ole massa Flint! I'm going roun' to aunt Marthy's to see 'bout it."

6   I bit my lips till the blood came to keep from crying out. Were my children with their grandmother, or had the speculator carried them off? The suspense was dreadful. Would Betty never come, and tell me the truth about it? At last she came, and I eagerly repeated what I had overheard. Her face was one broad, bright smile.

***

7   Great surprise was expressed when it was known that my children had returned to their grandmother's. The news spread through the town, and many a kind word was bestowed on the little ones.

8   Dr. Flint went to my grandmother's to ascertain who was the owner of my children, and she informed him. "I expected as much," said he. "I am glad to hear it. I have had news from Linda lately, and I shall soon have her. You need never expect to see her free. She shall be my slave as long as I live, and when I am dead she shall be the slave of my children. If I ever find out that you or Phillip had any thing to do with her running off I'll kill him. And if I meet William in the street, and he presumes to look at me, I'll flog him within an inch of his life. Keep those brats out of my sight!"

9   As he turned to leave, my grandmother said something to remind him of his own doings. He looked back upon her, as if he would have been glad to strike her to the ground.

10   I had my season of joy and thanksgiving. It was the first time since my childhood that I had experienced any real happiness. I heard of the old doctor's threats, but they no longer had the same power to trouble me. The darkest cloud that hung over my life had rolled away. Whatever slavery might do to me, it could not shackle my children. If I fell a sacrifice, my little ones were saved. It was well for me that my simple heart believed all that had been promised for their welfare. It is always better to trust than to doubt.

11   A small shed had been added to my grandmother's house years ago. Some boards were laid across the joists at the top, and between these boards and the roof was a very small garret, never occupied by anything but rats and mice. It was a pent roof, covered with nothing but shingles, according to the southern custom for such buildings. The garret was only nine feet long and seven wide. The highest part was three feet high, and sloped down abruptly to the loose board floor. There was no admission for either light or air. My uncle Phillip, who was a carpenter, had very skillfully made a concealed trap-door, which communicated with the storeroom. He had been doing this while I was waiting in the swamp. The storeroom opened upon a piazza. To this hole I was conveyed as soon as I entered the house. The air was stifling; the darkness total. A bed had been spread on the floor. I could sleep quite comfortably on one side; but the slope was so sudden that I could not turn on the other without hitting the roof. The rats and mice ran over my bed; but I was weary, and I slept such sleep as the wretched may, when a tempest has passed over them. Morning came. I knew it only by the noises I heard; for in my small den day and night were all the same. I suffered for air even more than for light. But I was not comfortless. I heard the voices of my children. There was joy and there was sadness in the sound. It made my tears flow. How I longed to speak to them! I was eager to look on their faces; but there was no hole, no crack, through which I could peep. This continued darkness was oppressive. It seemed horrible to sit or lie in a cramped position day after day, without one gleam of light. Yet I would have chosen this, rather than my lot as a slave, though white people considered it an easy one; and it was so compared with the fate of others. I was never cruelly overworked; I was never lacerated with the whip from head to foot; I was never so beaten and bruised that I could not turn from one side to the other; I never had my heel-strings cut to prevent my running away; I was never chained to a log and forced to drag it about, while I toiled in the fields from morning till night; I was never branded with hot iron, or torn by bloodhounds. On the contrary, I had

always been kindly treated, and tenderly cared for, until I came into the hands of Dr. Flint. I had never wished for freedom until then. But though my life in slavery was comparatively devoid of hardships, God pity the woman who is compelled to lead such a life!

12 My food was passed up to me through the trap-door my uncle had contrived; and my grandmother, my uncle Phillip, and aunt Nancy would seize such opportunities as they could, to mount up there and chat with me at the opening. But of course this was not safe in the daytime. It must all be done in darkness. It was impossible for me to move in an erect position, but I crawled about my den for exercise. One day I hit my head against something, and found it was a gimlet[2]. My uncle had left it sticking there when he made the trap-door. I was as rejoiced as Robinson Crusoe could have been at finding such a treasure. It put a lucky thought into my head. I said to myself, "Now I will have some light. Now I will see my children." I did not dare to begin my work during the daytime, for fear of attracting attention. But I groped round; and having found the side next the street, where I could frequently see my children, I stuck the gimlet in and waited for the evening. I bored three rows of holes, one above another; then I bored out the interstices between. I thus succeeded in making one hole about an inch long and an inch broad. I sat by it till late into the night, to enjoy the little whiff of air that floated in. In the morning I watched for my children. The first person I saw in the street was Dr. Flint. I had a shuddering, superstitious feeling that it was a bad omen. Several familiar faces passed by. At last I heard the merry laugh of children, and presently two sweet little faces were looking up at me, as though they knew I was there, and were conscious of the joy they imparted. How I longed to tell them I was there!

13 My condition was now a little improved. But for weeks I was tormented by hundreds of little red insects, fine as a needle's point, that pierced through my skin, and produced an intolerable burning. The good grandmother gave me herb teas and cooling medicines, and finally I got rid of them. The heat of my den was intense, for nothing but thin shingles protected me from the scorching summer's sun. But I had my consolations. Through my peeping-hole I could watch the children, and when they were near enough, I could hear their talk. . . . [Then] [a]utumn came, with a pleasant abatement of heat.

14 My eyes had become accustomed to the dim light, and by holding my book or work in a certain position near the aperture I contrived to read and sew. That was a great relief to the tedious monotony of my life. But when winter came, the cold penetrated through the thin shingle roof, and I was dreadfully chilled. The winters there are not so long, or so severe, as in northern latitudes; but the houses are not built to shelter from cold, and my little den was peculiarly comfortless. The kind grandmother brought me bed-clothes and warm drinks. Often I was obliged to lie in bed all day to keep comfortable; but with all my precautions, my shoulders and feet were frostbitten. O, those long, gloomy days, with no object for my eye to rest upon, and no thoughts to occupy my mind, except the dreary past and the uncertain future! I was thankful when there came a day sufficiently mild for me to wrap myself up and sit at the loophole to watch the passers-by. Southerners have the habit of stopping and talking in the streets, and I heard many conversations not intended to meet my ears. I heard slave-hunters planning how to catch some poor fugitive. Several times I heard allusions to Dr. Flint, myself, and the history of my children, who, perhaps, were playing near the gate. . . . The opinion was often expressed that I was in the Free States. Very rarely did any one suggest that I might be in the vicinity. Had the least suspicion rested on my grandmother's house, it would have been burned to the ground.

15 But it was the last place they thought of. Yet there was no place, where slavery existed, that could have afforded me so good a place of concealment.

16   Dr. Flint and his family repeatedly tried to coax and bribe my children to tell something they had heard said about me. One day the doctor took them into a shop, and offered them some bright little silver pieces and gay handkerchiefs if they would tell where their mother was. Ellen shrank away from him, and would not speak; but Benny spoke up, and said, "Dr. Flint, I don't know where my mother is. I guess she's in New York; and when you go there again, I wish you'd ask her to come home, for I want to see her; but if you put her in jail, or tell her you'll cut her head off, I'll tell her to go right back."

---

[1]speculator: a slave trader
[2]gimlet: a hand drill

21 What does <u>garret</u> mean in paragraph 11?

A. house

B. attic

C. bedroom

D. garage

22 The reader learns that the narrator's children have been freed from slavery when the narrator

A. overhears two women talking.

B. knows Dr. Flint in the house.

C. asks Betty what has happened.

D. sees them on the street.

23 In paragraph 10, the narrator says, "The darkest cloud that hung over my life had rolled away." This means that the narrator

A. was relieved.

B. felt angry.

C. could see.

D. was free.

24 The narrator is in danger because

A. she is desperate to see her children.

B. Betty has to open the trap door to bring her food.

C. Dr. Flint is still searching for her.

D. people outside can hear her talking.

25 Why did the narrator agree to be locked up in the garret?

A. It would keep her safe from Dr. Flint.

B. It would keep her out of trouble.

C. It would let her be closer to her children.

D. It would help her escape to New York.

26 Why aren't the narrator's children allowed to see her?

A. They might have to return to Dr. Flint.

B. They might give away her hiding place.

C. They might be sold again into slavery.

D. They might ask to be taken to the Free States.

27 What contributes MOST to the suspense of the story?

    A. the darkness of the room the narrator is in

    B. the innocence of the narrator's children

    C. how the narrator is forced to spend her time

    D. what might happen if the narrator is caught

28 The author's feelings toward Dr. Flint are caused by

    A. disbelief.

    B. fright.

    C. jealousy.

    D. misunderstanding.

29 In the first sentence, the hyphenated word "slave-traders" is used as

    A. an adjective.

    B. an adverb.

    C. a noun.

    D. a gerund.

Write your answer to open-response question 30 in the space provided in the Answer Sheets.

 30 In paragraph 11, the narrator says, "It was the first time since my childhood that I had experienced any real happiness."

- What has happened to make her happy?
- What might make her happy in the future?

Use information from the passage to support your answer.

LANGUAGE AND LITERATURE: SESSION 3

DIRECTIONS

This session contains two reading selections with multiple-choice questions and one open-response question. Mark your answers to these questions on the Answer Sheets provided.

Read the following poem and answer the questions that follow. As you read, think about the message the author is trying to convey.

Up-Hill

by Christina Rossetti

Does the road wind up-hill all the way?
    Yes, to the very end.
Will the day's journey take the whole long day?
    From morn to night my friend.

5 But is there for the night a resting-place?
    A roof for when the slow dark hours begin.
May not the darkness hide it from my face?
    You cannot miss that inn.

Shall I meet other wayfarers at night?
10   Those who have gone before.
Then must I knock, or call when just in sight?
    They will not keep you standing at that door.

Shall I find comfort, travel-sore and weak?
    Or labour you shall find the sum.
15 Will there be beds for me and all who seek?
    Yea, beds for all who come.

31 How long will the journey take?

A. one day

B. one week

C. the night

D. the morning

32 Who will the author meet at the inn?

A. the travel sore and weak

B. all those who have come before

C. those in need of a bed to rest

D. all those standing at the door

33 What is the tone of the poem?

A. scary

B. anxious

C. relieved

D. regretful

Write your answer to open-response question 34 in the space provided in the Answer Sheets.

34 What do you think the inn symbolizes? Use details from the poem in your answer.

Read the following dramatic adaptation and answer the questions that follow.

The Walker

Adapted from *You're Never Really Alone*
By Glenn Morrison

{**Scene:** An evening in early spring, on a quiet street. One man is walking quickly along, until he suddenly stops and stands still as if he were in a trance. Another man comes out onto his front porch a few yards from the sidewalk. He speaks to the first man.}

Cody: What's the matter, Boyce? You forget the way to work?

Boyce: No, man. Trying to decide whether I should *go* to work.

Cody: 'Course you got to go, "Blues Brother." How we get through the night 'less we hear you on the ray-dee-oh? You're a public servant, Boyce. Same as me. You got no choice, you see.

Boyce: C. W., your public service is driving the school bus. {He holds up his hand, the palm turned toward Cody.} Yeah, I appreciate it's an honorable and necessary job. But you know you don't stay up to listen to my show.

Cody: Brother Boyce, knowing that you are there is enough. Besides there are nights some evil keep a man awake. Bad stomach, you see. A deep discussion with the old lady. Gracie has her opinions. I go downstairs, put your station on. Listen to a cut from Champion Jack Dupree, Muddy Waters, Cool Breeze Monroe, like that. Frees the hurt, calms the spirit. A man can go back to rest, you see.

Boyce: I understand blues in the night, man. We all have souls that need to rest.

Cody: Amen to that. Gracie, she listens to your last hour in the morning. She has to get up at five, you see, to be on duty at the hospital. Your music gets her in the swing of the day, she says. Don't have to listen to those hog and beans reports.

Boyce: Ok, C.W., suppose I play some Bessie Smith this morning for your lady. About 5:30.

Cody: Oh, you *are* going to work. Very fine. She'll listen. Well then go. I've got to get inside. Catch a cold out here. People depend on me, too, you see.

{Cody goes back into his house and the porch door slams behind him. With that sharp sound, Boyce turns back, heaves a sigh, and continues on his quick-paced walk.}

35 What kind of work does Boyce do?

A. TV reporter.

B. Late night radio disk jockey.

C. Teacher.

D. Something in the hospital.

36 Cody and his wife Gracie

A. rely on farm reports to do their jobs.

B. sleep late on work days.

C. work at the same place.

D. argue at times.

37 How is Cody's attitude toward his job different from Boyce's?

A. Cody believes he performs a necessary public service.

B. Cody wishes he made more money.

C. Boyce would rather work outside like Cody.

D. They have the same attitude and opinions.

38 The author lets us know this is a friendly conversation by

A. the body language of the two men.

B. the attitude they have about work.

C. the nicknames they use for each other.

D. the feelings they have for their wives.

39 What could you do to apply Cody's method of getting back to sleep in the middle of the night?

A. Read a book or watch TV.

B. Eat something.

C. Wake up somebody and talk with them.

D. Work around the house.

40 The author has Cody repeatedly use the phrase "you see" to

A. add to Cody's distinctive personality

B. show that Cody is annoyed with Boyce.

C. show that Cody thinks Boyce doesn't understand him.

D. suggest that Boyce is still in a trance-like state.

ANSWER SHEETS

Part B: Language and Literature

SESSION 1

1. Ⓐ Ⓑ Ⓒ Ⓓ

2. Ⓐ Ⓑ Ⓒ Ⓓ

3. Ⓐ Ⓑ Ⓒ Ⓓ

4. Ⓐ Ⓑ Ⓒ Ⓓ

5. Ⓐ Ⓑ Ⓒ Ⓓ

6. Ⓐ Ⓑ Ⓒ Ⓓ

7. _____

   _____

   _____

   _____

   _____

   _____

   _____

8. Ⓐ Ⓑ Ⓒ Ⓓ

9. Ⓐ Ⓑ Ⓒ Ⓓ

10. Ⓐ Ⓑ Ⓒ Ⓓ

11. Ⓐ Ⓑ Ⓒ Ⓓ

12. Ⓐ Ⓑ Ⓒ Ⓓ

13. Ⓐ   Ⓑ   Ⓒ   Ⓓ

14. _____

    _____

    _____

    _____

    _____

    _____

    _____

15. Ⓐ   Ⓑ   Ⓒ   Ⓓ

16. Ⓐ   Ⓑ   Ⓒ   Ⓓ

17. Ⓐ   Ⓑ   Ⓒ   Ⓓ

18. Ⓐ   Ⓑ   Ⓒ   Ⓓ

19. Ⓐ   Ⓑ   Ⓒ   Ⓓ

20. Ⓐ   Ⓑ   Ⓒ   Ⓓ

SESSION 2

21. Ⓐ   Ⓑ   Ⓒ   Ⓓ

22. Ⓐ   Ⓑ   Ⓒ   Ⓓ

23. Ⓐ   Ⓑ   Ⓒ   Ⓓ

24. Ⓐ   Ⓑ   Ⓒ   Ⓓ

25. Ⓐ   Ⓑ   Ⓒ   Ⓓ

26. Ⓐ   Ⓑ   Ⓒ   Ⓓ

27. Ⓐ   Ⓑ   Ⓒ   Ⓓ

28. Ⓐ   Ⓑ   Ⓒ   Ⓓ

29. Ⓐ   Ⓑ   Ⓒ   Ⓓ

30. _____

_____

_____

_____

_____

_____

_____

SESSION 3

31. Ⓐ   Ⓑ   Ⓒ   Ⓓ

32. Ⓐ   Ⓑ   Ⓒ   Ⓓ

33. Ⓐ   Ⓑ   Ⓒ   Ⓓ

34. _____

_____

_____

_____

_____

_____

35. Ⓐ   Ⓑ   Ⓒ   Ⓓ

36. Ⓐ   Ⓑ   Ⓒ   Ⓓ

37. Ⓐ   Ⓑ   Ⓒ   Ⓓ

38. Ⓐ   Ⓑ   Ⓒ   Ⓓ

39. Ⓐ   Ⓑ   Ⓒ   Ⓓ

40. Ⓐ   Ⓑ   Ⓒ   Ⓓ

ANSWER KEY

Part A

WRITING: SESSIONS 1 AND 2

Sample answer:

To the City Council:

I have just learned of your plans to cut down the oak tree in the center of town square. The thought of losing another historical landmark of our town saddens me. The old oak tree has been a part of so many lives. When my great-grandparents got married, they were photographed under the old oak. We have pictures of my grandmother and grandfather as toddlers swinging from the branches. They too were photographed there on their wedding day, as were my parents. On my bedroom wall, I have a photograph of my best friend and me attempting to climb the massive tree when we were barely old enough to walk. Obviously, this tree has been around for many generations, and I always hoped that one day my own children would get to experience the joy of sitting under the old oak on a hot, summer day.

I understand that one reason given for the removal of the tree is that the branches might impede the poles and wires. It's never been a problem for city workers to trim these branches before. Why is it a problem now? I think the bigger issue is that you want to build a movie theater to bring in more money. The last thing this town needs is another movie theater. We already have a cinema at each end of town. Is it really necessary to add another? These massive buildings, with their long lines and gaudy lights, detract from the natural beauty of our town. Why destroy the one glorious work of nature we have left? I urge you to think very carefully before you plow under another historical landmark.

Part B

LANGUAGE AND LITERATURE: SESSION 1

1. **C** (Understanding a Text)

   Grandfather says that he does not think it's a good idea for him to review Enrico's story because it's sometimes difficult to accept criticism and he would not want to hurt Enrico's feelings.

2. **B** (Vocabulary Development)

   When Grandfather says "No, no, Enrico, don't do that," he is correcting Enrico. "Correcting" and "chiding" have nearly the same meaning.

3. **A** (Understanding a Text)

   Grandfather says that he predicted the outcome of Enrico's story after reading the first paragraph. Therefore, answer choice A is the correct answer.

4. **B** (Reading/Fiction)

   Enrico says "ouch!" when Grandfather criticizes his short story. The title "Ouch!" describes how Enrico feels when Grandfather tells him what is wrong with his story.

5.   D   (Reading/Fiction)

Enrico is appreciative of the many different ways his grandfather helps him. You can also eliminate incorrect answer choices to find the correct answer to this question.

6.   C   (Style and Language)

The author uses dialogue to convey the theme or central idea in this story. The author does not use repetition, personification, or flashback in this story.

7.   (Reading/Fiction)

Sample answer: The author included this detail to show that Grandfather was very intelligent and had a great deal of experience writing. This makes him an authority on the subject and experienced enough to guide Enrico in the right direction. This relates to the central idea of the story because Enrico wants to be a writer and turns to Grandfather for guidance.

8.   B   (Understanding a Text)

The author says that because of a decrease in spending, many cities are lacking art. Therefore, answer choice B is the correct answer.

9.   B   (Vocabulary Development)

The author says theater companies have packed up their productions and vacated their theaters. This means they left the theaters.

10.   D   (Reading/Nonfiction)

The type of art the author refers to in the article is not popular culture. Answer choices A, B, and C are types of popular culture as described in the article. Answer choice D is the correct answer.

11.   C   (Reading/Nonfiction)

The author uses convincing language throughout the article. He or she is trying to persuade readers of the importance of increased funding for the arts. Answer choice C is the correct answer.

12.   C   (Understanding a Text)

The main idea of the article is that we need to increase government funding for the arts. Answer choice C, "Communities suffer when they lose artists," best supports this idea.

13.   **A**   (Style and Language)

"Twenty-something" and "middle-aged" are adjectives modifying "adults."

14.   (Reading/Nonfiction)

Sample answer: While most states would probably like to increase their funding of the arts, there just isn't enough money to do so. While the arts are an important part of culture, extra money should be spent helping people in need. In some cities, there are more pressing issues than the arts, such as improving schools and providing food and shelter for the homeless. A person who would likely oppose funding for the arts is a business person who wants a city to prosper financially and wants to invest money in areas that may make more money.

15.   **A**   (Developing Vocabulary)

The article says that you can create a safe and healthy habitat for your fish. Answer choice A, environment, is the best answer choice.

16.   **C**   (Reading/Nonfiction)

This question asks you to conclude who probably wrote the advertisement. "Salesperson" is the best answer choice since the advertisement is trying to sell supplies.

17.   **B**   (Reading/Nonfiction)

The paragraph says, " . . . you don't have to settle for anything less than the best" and that they carry "top brand names." Therefore answer choice B is the best answer.

18.   **B**   (Reading/Nonfiction)

The author begins the passage with a question to get readers' attention. Answer choice B is the correct answer. The other answer choices do not really apply to this passage.

19.   **B**   (Style and Language)

The author has a humorous tone. He refers to fish as "flippered friends" and says they will not gnaw furniture, shred curtains, or shed fur.

20.   **A**   (Understanding a Text)

To answer this question, you have to look at the ad. Since a fish tank starts at $19.99, it is the most expensive item.

LANGUAGE AND LITERATURE: SESSION 2

21.   B   (Developing Vocabulary)

The sentence in paragraph 12 that uses the word "garret" says, "Some boards were laid across the joists at the top, and between these boards and the roof was a very small garret, never occupied by anything but rats and mice." This sentence describes a floor over a building but under the roof, so the correct answer is B: attic.

22.   C   (Understanding a Text)

The narrator has a vision or a dream about her children. Then she hears two women talking about them, but she is still not sure what happened, so she asks Betty.

23.   A   (Reading/Fiction)

This question asks you to interpret a figurative term. The narrator says she feels like a dark cloud had just rolled out of her life. Considering that she said this after learning her children were free from slavery, we can understand that she was relieved. Answer choice A is correct.

24.   C   (Understanding a Text)

The narrator has many dangers in her life, but once she is hidden away, she is safer. At that time, the greatest danger she faces is that Dr. Flint is still searching for her. He questions people, including her own family, on her whereabouts, and vows to recapture her.

25.   A   (Understanding a Text)

Although the narrator's life in hiding is difficult, she agrees to it because it will keep her safe from Dr. Flint. Dr. Flint makes it well known that he wants to hunt her down and recapture her. She feels that hiding in the garret is preferable to being made a slave again.

26.   B   (Understanding a Text)

All through the excerpt, the narrator was desperate to see her children again. However, she was unable to do so because if they went to visit her in her hiding place, she might be discovered by the authorities or Dr. Flint.

27.   D   (Reading/Fiction)

There are several reasons that a story like this is suspenseful. However, the best reason is that the reader doesn't know what will happen to the narrator if she's captured. Therefore, answer choice D is the best answer.

28.   B   (Reading/Fiction)

The narrator relates that Dr. Flint was a cruel and vicious man. She says that she had always been treated decently until she "came into the hands of Dr. Flint." It is clear that she was afraid of again becoming his slave.

29.   C   (Style and Language)

"Slave-traders" is used here as a noun.

30.   (Reading/Fiction)

Sample answer: The narrator has learned that her children are now free from slavery and Dr. Flint, and this has made her very happy. She says that whatever slavery might do to her, it can no longer touch her children. She would be extremely happy in the future if she were allowed to be reunited with her children.

LANGUAGE AND LITERATURE: SESSION 3

31.   A   (Understanding a Text)

In the first stanza of the poem, the speaker says the journey will take from morning until night. One day is the correct answer.

32.   B   (Understanding a Text)

The poem says the author will meet all those who have come before. Answer choice B is correct.

33.   C   (Reading/Poetry)

The poem is not scary and the speaker does not seem regretful or especially anxious. She does seem tired and relieved to hear the answers to her questions. Answer choice C is correct.

34.   (Reading/Poetry)

Sample answer: The inn symbolizes death. It is the end of the road. This is why the author will see all those who have come before and will find comfort at last.

35.   B   (Understanding a Text)

Boyce is a late-night disk jockey, playing old-time blues music.

36.   D   (Understanding a Text)

Cody and Gracie work at different early-morning jobs, neither of which relies on farm reports. They argue from time to time, as married people sometimes do.

37.   A   (Reading/Drama)

Cody believes he performs a necessary public service and tries to convince Boyce that he does also.

38.   C   (Reading/Drama)

The friendly nicknames they use help identify this as a good-natured conversation.

39.   A   (Reading/Drama)

You might watch TV or read to get the same result as Cody does listening to Boyce on the radio, without disturbing anyone.

40.   A   (Style and Language)

The repetition of "you see" is just part of Cody's unique personality. He says it without thinking, the way some people say "you know."

NOTES